T0281768

Praise for *Midnight in Ironbottom Sound*

"Dead in the water, with her deck a tangle of flames, the USS *Gregory*'s fate on September 5, 1942, was quickly sealed. *Midnight in Ironbottom Sound* offers a gripping reconstruction of the destroyer's final moments, as well as important insight into the officers and crew that fought for survival. This riveting true story is filled with surprise twists—both what transpired during the war and what was finally resolved seventy-seven years later. Charles Jackson French is a hero for the ages. I'm so glad Avriett unearthed this never-before-told World War II story. It desperately needed to be brought to light."

—Marcus Brotherton, *New York Times* bestselling author

"A gripping story of heroism on the watery WWII battlefields of the Pacific. Carole Engle Avriett takes us along on the High Speed Transport USS *Gregory* and the fateful naval battle that added the *Gregory* to the infamous Ironbottom Sound. This riveting drama, told through personal narratives with an historian's eye and a storyteller's soul, examines what it means to be a leader, a warrior, and a hero."

—John A. Dailey, author of *Tough, Rugged Bastards: A Memoir of a Life in Marine Special Operations*

"My late grandfather was an early advocate of the APDs and their use in reconnaissance, raids, and other special operations of Marine Raiders, especially Edson's Raiders. The dedication and sacrifice made by the officers and crews of the APDs were an indispensable part in winning the Guadalcanal campaign and the war. *Midnight in Ironbottom Sound* finally tells their story, and is sure to be a favorite for readers who love military history."

—Merritt A. Edson III, grandson of Maj. Gen. Merritt Edson of the legendary battalion known as Edson's Raiders

"Tales of sacrifice and courage about the men who fought in the South Pacific during the Second World War aboard the USS *Gregory* will continue to influence future generations. My Uncle Harry will always stand as my link to the Greatest Generation, and I'm proud that his story will continue to inspire."

—Bryan Condra, great-nephew of Harry F. Bauer,
Commander of the USS *Gregory*

"It's nice to see Charles French finally getting the recognition he deserves. He was a true hero."

—Chester French, nephew of Charles Jackson French

MIDNIGHT IN IRONBOTTOM SOUND

MIDNIGHT IN IRONBOTTOM SOUND

The Harrowing WWII Story of Heroism in the Shark-Infested Waters of Guadalcanal

CAROLE ENGLE AVRIETT

Foreword by Cedric E. Pringle, Rear Admiral USN (Ret.)

REGNERY
HISTORY

Copyright © 2024 by Carole Engle Avriett
Foreword copyright © 2024 by Cedric E. Pringle

All rights reserved. No part of this book may be reproduced in any manner without the express written consent of the publisher, except in the case of brief excerpts in critical reviews or articles. All inquiries should be addressed to Regnery History, 307 West 36th Street, 11th Floor, New York, NY 10018.

Regnery History books may be purchased in bulk at special discounts for sales promotion, corporate gifts, fund-raising, or educational purposes. Special editions can also be created to specifications. For details, contact the Special Sales Department, Regnery History, 307 West 36th Street, 11th Floor, New York, NY 10018 or info@skyhorsepublishing.com.

Regnery® is a registered trademark and its colophon is a trademark of Skyhorse Publishing Inc.®, a Delaware corporation.

Visit our website at www.regnery.com.
Please follow our publisher Tony Lyons on Instagram @tonylyonsisuncertain.

10 9 8 7 6 5 4 3 2 1

Library of Congress Cataloging-in-Publication Data

Names: Avriett, Carole Engle, author.
Title: Midnight in Ironbottom Sound : the harrowing WWII story of heroism
   in the shark-infested waters of Guadalcanal / Carole Engle Avriett.
Other titles: Harrowing WWII story of heroism in the shark-infested waters
   of Guadalcanal
Description: New York, NY : Regnery History, [2024] | Includes
   bibliographical references and index. | Summary: "A captivating WW II
   narrative set in the Pacific"-- Provided by publisher.
Identifiers: LCCN 2024025282 | ISBN 9781510781597 (hardcover) | ISBN
   9781510781757 (epub)
Subjects: LCSH: Guadalcanal, Battle of, Solomon Islands, 1942-1943. |
   Gregory (Destroyer) | Little (Destroyer : APD-4) | Bauer, Harry F.,
   1904-1942. | World War, 1939-1945--Pacific Area. | World War,
   1939-1945--Naval operations, American. | French, Charles J., 1919-1956.
   | United States. Navy--Biography.
Classification: LCC D774.G83 A97 2024 | DDC
   940.54/265933--dc23/eng/20240611
LC record available at https://lccn.loc.gov/2024025282

Cover design by John Caruso

Print ISBN: 978-1-5107-8159-7
eBook ISBN: 978-1-5107-8175-7

Printed in the United States of America

For my wonderful husband, Louis, who loved his time in the Navy as a dentist, especially when stationed at Marine Corps Air Station in Beaufort, South Carolina.

The book is also for my father, who spent twenty-five years in the Navy and was on duty at Pearl Harbor on December 7, 1941.

Most of all this book is in honor of the American sailors who went to war in the Solomon Islands: almost three times as many died at sea defending Guadalcanal as Marines and Army personnel died on it.

Contents

Foreword

"Let this ship inspire us to challenge our own limitations and to always—always—answer the call of duty, even when the waters are rough and the path ahead uncertain."
—The Honorable Carlos Del Toro, Secretary of the Navy, Surface Navy Symposium, January 10, 2024

It is with deep honor and humility that I write the foreword for this book that captures the selfless service of Lieutenant Commander Harry F. Bauer, commanding officer of USS *Gregory* (APD-3), and Petty Officer Charles J. French, the ship's heroic mess steward whose valiant actions during World War II continue to inspire service members today.

Upon reading Carole Avriett's previous book, *Marine Raiders: The True Story of the Legendary WWII Battalions*, there were three things that immediately became crystal clear to me. First, Carole is a phenomenal historian and engaging storyteller. She takes the reader on an enlightening and emotional journey through each scene while displaying the gallant actions of the Marines and Sailors of the Marine Raider Battalions and the Navy ships that supported them. Carole conveys their efforts and sacrifices which were vital to the Allied victory in the Pacific Theater and, more importantly, she displays the human elements of conflict in a way that we can all appreciate. This book represents the next logical step by telling the story primarily from the maritime point of view, while focusing on the perspectives of the Ship's Captain and Petty Officer French.

Second, I was reminded that sea duty provides a unique perspective and strengthens the bonds between all who sail into harm's way. In February 2012, I had the pleasure of serving as the 3rd Commanding Officer of USS *Makin Island* (LHD-8) and earned the call sign "Raider 3" by taking command of one of the Navy's newest ships in the fleet. Our ship was the second to be named after the famous 1942 Makin Island raid and the first ship to feature some of the most innovative propulsion technologies in recent history. The hybrid gas turbine and electric drive system was revolutionary at the time, and has since become the propulsion system of choice for many newer ships.

However, a ship is only as good as its crew. We were fortunate to have many plank owners who had been with the ship prior to her commissioning in 2009, as well as those of us who arrived prior to workups and deployment. We were also fortunate that each crewmember shared a relationship with Carlson's Raiders of the 2nd Marine Raider Battalion, and that leaders at all levels used Raider stories as motivation to continuously innovate and improve. During my time onboard, we lived by the Raider motto "Gung Ho," which means "to work together." One of my favorite mantras was "Excellence is a journey, not a destination," which became crucial to building our culture of excellence. We concluded each all-hands call and every awards ceremony with a loud "Team Raider" cheer as a nod to our namesake. For warfare qualifications, each Sailor had to know our ship's history as well as they knew our ship's mission.

When we departed San Diego, California, as the Makin Island Amphibious Ready Group with Amphibious Squadron Five (PHIBRON 5) and nearly 2,000 Marines from the 11th Marine Expeditionary Unit (11th MEU) embarked, we were ready to successfully complete every mission throughout our seven-month deployment, regardless of expected and unexpected challenges. Although we experienced our fair share of adversity, mostly due to exploring the limits and nuances of our new technology, we were blessed not to face any major conflicts or combat.

However, like the crew of the USS *Gregory*, we did everything in our power to maximize our readiness while helping the Marines prepare for whatever tasks faced them ashore. The Marines of 11th MEU reciprocated by fully integrating with our ship's gun crews during transits through the world's chokepoints, when ships are most vulnerable to attack. Doing so made USS *Makin Island* a hard target and served as a deterrent to any potential adversary, while strengthening the bonds between our Blue/Green Team. Following our deployment, we earned numerous unit, fleet, and Navy level awards for excellence in Battle Efficiency, Warfighting Readiness, Operational Safety, Food Service, Retention, and Energy Conservation. Our esprit de corps was unmatched, and the Raider culture of excellence continues today.

Third and last, while writing this foreword, I was reminded by the Honorable Carlos Del Toro, Secretary of the Navy, that acts of honor, courage, and commitment are eternal. On January 10, 2024, SECNAV announced that the name of our newest destroyer, DDG 142, will be the USS *Charles J. French*. Petty Officer French's actions following the Imperial Japanese attack on the USS *Gregory* are well-documented. In the aftermath, French rescued fifteen shipmates by gathering them onto a raft and, fearing they would drift to a Japanese-controlled island, swimming to a different island while towing the raft through shark-infested waters. Although he was recommended for the Navy Cross for his actions, he was presented a letter of commendation. Thank you, Mr. Secretary, for properly recognizing Petty Officer French's service.

Many more details of the courageous acts of Petty Officer French, Lieutenant Commander Bauer, and other members of the USS *Gregory* are captured on the following pages. This is certainly an inspirational story that should be read by leaders and applied to inspire teams to challenge our limitations. May we forever remember the crew of USS *Gregory* as the consummate American heroes who put service above self. The nation remains dedicated to honoring their courage and selflessness for generations to come. We are stronger together!

—Cedric "Raider 3" Pringle, Rear Admiral (Retired),
United States Navy Former Commanding Officer,
USS *Makin Island* (LHD-8)

Author's Note

Special thanks to the family of Robert Nelson Adrian: Captain, USN, and World War II veteran, for sharing his personal journals filled with eyewitness accounts of these events.

And congratulations to the family of Charles Jackson French: the Secretary of the Navy, Carlos del Toro, has recently announced that a destroyer of the Arleigh Burke class will be named for this true hero from WWII.

> "Greater love has no one than this, that someone lay down his life for his friends."
>
> —John 15:13

As with most narratives of WWII stories written today, nearly all characters are deceased . . . and authors must rely on a multitude of alternative sources.

After four years of research delving into personal memoirs of eyewitnesses who were actually on the USS *Gregory*, most notably those of Robert Adrian, plus diaries, published autobiographies, letters, contemporary newspaper and magazine articles, oral histories, military records, and many hours of interviews with family members of those who participated in these stories, I can say with confidence that the depiction here of what transpired is as authentic as possible. Though tapes of original conversations or brief speeches may not exist, the content of what is presented is consistent with documented events.

Occasionally dialogue, thoughts and emotions are imagined, based on what characters likely would have said/thought/felt in real time and suggested by written descriptions from eyewitnesses or family members familiar with events.

Fortunately, two major incidents, the hellish night during the battle in Ironbottom Sound and subsequent circumstances on shore, were clearly recorded in detail in later years by Robert Adrian (Capt. USN,) who was a shipmate on the *Gregory*. In addition, multiple interviews with present-day active duty and retired Navy personnel and Marine Raiders provided real-life insights into daily life at sea and during surface engagements.

Since all of the main characters portrayed in this book are no longer living, we will never have a continuous bridge we can traverse in order to know these brave and sacrificial warriors personally. However, what we *do* have are reliable stepping stones which point us, nonetheless, to their awe-inspiring bravery and courage, their willingness to give everything for their country. More importantly, these stepping stones provide us an opportunity to learn about their deeds so we can remember and honor them, heroes all, with humble gratitude for their service.

Part I

Introduction

"The Solomon Islands campaign is a unique and fascinating chapter in Naval history. Covering a period of seventeen months in 1942–43, it was marked by unremitting warfare, by sudden and vicious surface engagements, most of them at night, most at very close range, and all of them deadly. It will never be repeated, and those who took part will never forget it."[*]

This is the true story of one of those engagements, labeled "minor" by naval historians and, if mentioned, usually *in paren*—of a little-known ship crewed by unknown sailors caught up in a disastrous night of terror . . . and minor to all except those who were there.

Among myriad stories from World War II it's sometimes the seemingly inconsequential events which tell the tale best: of bravery beyond limits, sacrifice without conditions. This is the story of young men in their brave "little" ship designated an APD (Auxiliary Personnel/ Destroyer) who exemplified honor under the most nightmarish conditions: their mission, to deliver Marine Raiders to bloody beaches deep in the South Pacific at the beginning of WWII.

In particular, two of the gallant sailors on the USS *Gregory*—the highest ranking, who commanded the ship, Harry F. Bauer, and one of the lowest ranking, a mess attendant 2nd class named Charles Jackson French—reveal a mostly unknown story. These men along with their shipmates, who included a young ensign who witnessed it all, define one eternal truth: courage has no color, no prerequisites . . . Valor hails from within.

---

[*] Newcomb, Richard F., *The Battle of Savo Island*, New York: Henry Holt, 1961, vii.

1

CHAPTER 1

Midnight in Hell's Waters

"Then I said to you, 'Do not be in dread or afraid of them. The LORD your God who goes before you will Himself fight for you . . .'" Deuteronomy 1:29–30

September 5, 1942

The mess attendant swam rapidly with powerful strokes in the midnight waters towards the bobbing rubber raft. Behind Charles Jackson French, out-of-control fires from his ship, the USS *Gregory*, and pounding explosions continued to erupt, creating ghostly reflections all around him. Sounds of men screaming in agony and shouting for help could be heard everywhere. When he reached the raft, he realized there were several badly wounded sailors inside. He pulled himself in. Soon, another sailor splashed up to the craft's side.

"Is that you, French?" spit out the ship's young ensign, Bob Adrian, with great difficulty. Adrian's face was badly cut and bleeding. His right eye was shut tightly.

"Yessir, it's me," gasped French. "You okay, Sir? Them enemy ships got the jump on us!"

"They did indeed," Adrian said, coughing between words. "Let's try to get this raft further away from the ship. Looks like the *Gregory*'s going down! Thank God we got all those Raiders landed on Guadalcanal before this happened!"

After French slid back into the water, the two men strained to pull the raft, holding on with one arm and using the other to dog-paddle

3

through the water and away from the flaming ships. They could see the sister ship of the *Gregory*, the USS *Little*, in the distance, also racked with tremendous explosions and engulfed in flames.

Back on the *Gregory*, crew members were trying to get their beloved commander, Harry Frederick Bauer, into the water and away from the ship. He was badly wounded; both legs appeared broken, but he was still conscious. As the sailors reached him where he was lying on one of the few spots not engulfed with flames, they heard another man not far from where they were, screaming for help. At the same time, they could feel the ship begin slowly rolling to one side.

The men who were already in the water saw what was happening. French and Adrian had pulled the raft far enough away that they were out of danger from being sucked down with it—they hoped. Exhausted, especially Adrian who had a badly wounded leg, the shipmates decided to climb into the raft to catch their breath. The handful of sailors who were already on board were in terrible shape, most groaning in pain due to shrapnel wounds and burns.

Suddenly, machine gun bullets were whizzing through the air not far from where they were. They could hear sailors yelling and thrashing in the water, some pleading for their lives. They looked at each other, knowing what the Japanese were doing. "Damn'em," growled French, gazing into the chaos of fire and blackness.

After a few seconds French muttered, "Didja see Cap'n Bauer get off the ship?"

"No," answered Adrian. "Maybe he's somewhere behind us."

"Hope so . . . sure hope so . . ." French's voice trailed off, thinking about Lieutenant Commander Harry Bauer, the *Gregory*'s skipper. He had had a congenial relationship with the commander, a man nearly twenty years his senior.

About that time, there was an eerie scraping sound under the raft, then a bump strong enough to partially lift one side. French and Adrian froze. A few seconds later, they felt another sinister grinding across the bottom.

The young men stared out over the pandemonium—they knew another type of predator had now discovered them. Soon they saw dorsal fins, backlit by the fires cutting through the waters all around them.

"We're in a hella'va mess," said Bob Adrian, who slumped beside French.

"Yessiree," answered the young mess attendant, shaking his head slowly back and forth. "You can say that again."

Fifty Years Later: September 5, 1992

Sailor Bob Adrian deftly descended the twisting, narrow stairs emptying into a dimly lit passageway. With long, quick strides, he reached his small, ten-by-ten-foot cabin where a black wraparound desk filled one corner, and a small bunk the other. He pulled the string, clicking on the ceiling light bulb. Off to the side, a compact area with a sign above the door labeled HEAD provided Adrian a place to shower and shave. An old space heater helped warm the dark, damp area. Bare bones.

Dropping down into the well-worn desk chair, Bob Adrian fastidiously cleaned his pipe, then lit up a special blend of cherry vanilla tobacco, made especially for him at his favorite smoke shop. He sat still for several minutes, eyes closed, enjoying these first few puffs. He could sense a gentle ocean beneath his cabin, rocking him back and forth, knowing it could change later in the day. His thoughts turned to the ship and crew . . . and . . .

Suddenly, from somewhere in the distance above him, he heard someone tapping on a ceiling pipe, then a voice calling.

"Dad? Hey, Dadoo . . . are you down there?" It was his daughter, Judy, signaling that his wife, Joan, had lunch ready.

After Robert Nelson Adrian's retirement from the Navy with the rank of captain, this basement room in his three-story home just a block from his beloved Naval Academy had become his personal wardroom, his retreat, his command center: a shrine. Pictures of ships, sailors, ports of call filled every square inch of wall. Three large portraits, one of Fleet Admiral William D. Leahy, one of four-star Admiral Ulysses S. Grant Sharp Jr., and one of Admiral Arleigh Burke, all of whom Bob had served with, dignified the plethora of memorabilia. The room—just like its occupant—was pure Navy.

However, the appeal of a basement room had even deeper roots for Bob than a place to keep memorabilia from his nearly twenty-five years in the Navy. His early youth and teenage years loosely paralleled the growing depression across the country and the world. His dad's sheep operation had become increasingly difficult and other business ventures floundered. As the family struggled to stay afloat, the young boy with his mom and dad had lived for different periods of time in various places—small apartments, hotels, a front office with a room and john in the back, tents, and at one point, when they were in a tiny one-bedroom house, Bob slept on a screened-in back porch. Finally, when he was a junior in high school, his dad was able to provide a three-bedroom house for the family.

"It was my first-ever real bedroom," remembered Bob, smiling. "I was so excited—and it was in the basement!"

Over the years in this present ship-like, spartan space, Bob journaled and recorded events from a lifetime filled with service. But most importantly, he would mull over those gripping memories produced by many months of WWII engagements in the treacherous waters of the South Pacific. All of them were major, but some incidents remained more vivid and paramount than others.

This day on the calendar was one of those days. Fifty years before, on the fifth day of September in 1942, Bob, then a young ensign, had been on the USS *Gregory* when she came under vicious attacks one dark, terrible night in the dangerous waters off Guadalcanal. Their sole purpose in those waters was to transport and deliver Marine Raiders from one bloody beach to another. Though vital and indispensable to the war effort, these brave ships and crews were essentially unknown, and remain so even today.

What transpired through all those hellish hours stayed with Bob Adrian. He remembered with fondness and awe so many of the men he had served with, yet two would continue to be at the forefront of his recollections of his very first duty assignment in the Navy: Harry Bauer and Charles Jackson French. Bauer had been his commanding officer on the USS *Gregory* and French one of her mess attendants.

Bob thought back to the NBC broadcast he had done that same year, 1942. After he returned to the States, he was interviewed and shared these stories with a listening nation. He went over again in his mind the deadly attacks, when he had been so terrified, badly wounded, and witnessed Bauer and French do some of the bravest things he had ever seen. On this same day, September 5, every year since, he remembered the *Gregory* and all her crew—but especially these two outstanding, courageous men.

The retired captain placed his pipe in the heavy brass ashtray marked Navy Issue and headed upstairs to the kitchen. "Bauer and French," he thought to himself, shaking his head. "Such incredibly different men but alike in subtle, yet critical ways."

CHAPTER 2

Dangerous Waters, Part 1

"When you pass through the waters, I will be with you;
and through the rivers, they shall not overwhelm you . . ."
Isaiah 43:2

It's no small boast to claim that someone's great swimming prowess began in a legendary river: a waterway dubbed "The Meanest River" by locals, or sometimes after a drowning, of which there have been many, their cruder moniker for it, "Bitch River." Horses and cattle die in the exact spot where, ensnared by its deep, sucking sandy bottom, they are rendered powerless to struggle free. Casual swimmers find themselves pulled under, helpless in its swirling undercurrents. Bodies are seldom found.

Eclipsed only by the Mississippi, the Red River's richly layered history frames much of the story of the Great American West, largely due to its length and location. Its headwaters of small rivulets and fingerlings originate near Tucumcari, New Mexico. They merge into a flowing river just south of Amarillo in the Texas Panhandle, which defines the border between Texas and Oklahoma. Continuing eastward, the river's strong, surging waters drag along mud from loose red clay banks, branches, and logs, carrying the mixture all the way to Arkansas. There it forms a big bend turning south through Louisiana, eventually joining the confluence of the Mississippi River—over 1,300 miles of perilous red water—smelly, unpredictable, and potentially dangerous the whole way.

Throughout the 1800s, estimates suggest more than ten million cattle and one million horses crossed through its water, never without incident. The Trail of Tears ended at its edge. It has inspired songwriters, novelists, and filmmakers, including Howard Hawkes's 1948 classic, *Red River*, in which John Wayne portrays a trail boss driving nine thousand Texas cattle northward across these iconic waters.

Of the five states the Red River flows through or borders, it shares the least amount of real estate with Arkansas. For a small distance the river forms the border between Texas and Arkansas, before plunging eastward to form a large, significant bend that reorients the river's course directly south towards Shreveport.

The land east of the border and before this enormous river bend is known as the Red River Bottoms—verdant, rich, and called by some "the river's charm and value." This bottomland for decades supported fields of cotton, pecan orchards, wheat, and rye, spreading as far as the eye could see over miles and miles of maroon dirt. Dozens of sharecroppers built small clapboard houses where they reared large families and farmed rich land.

In these bottoms the cotton industry thrived, and the nearby small town of Foreman, Arkansas, bustled in the early 1900s. Cotton gins hummed, a railroad track ran through the middle of downtown, and a movie theater, shops, and a few cafes serving southern cooking at its finest kept a lively atmosphere. For children growing up in the Bottoms, the occasional trip to town was like a visit to a theme park.

Nevertheless, the Red River dominated the land and, from a certain perspective, the people as well. Living out in the Bottoms, children found play among trees and swampy areas and, when daring enough, even in the river. But they were all well aware of its reputation.

"Them's dangerous waters, child—don't you be going down there in them waters." If the skinny little Arkansas boy, small for his age from birth on September 25, 1919, had heard that admonishment once from his elders, he'd heard it a million times. Everyone knew the dangers inherent in the Red River.

Maybe that's why the youngster just *had* to do it—to go down into the waters and see for himself. Maybe he felt an inherent need to prove something. He had always been small for his age, often picked on by the other boys, and had learned early to stand up for himself or be run over. Or maybe it was simply a child's adventurous spirit being told *don't* once too often, and *do* was the only remedy.

Whatever the case, eight-year-old Charles Jackson French ventured out into the Red River one sunny afternoon. At first, he waded in only ankle-deep. He could feel the incredibly soft silt beneath his feet. It wasn't quicksand, but the effect was very similar. He sank down to mid-calf, then had to force his feet up before stepping down again. He was now in about two feet of muddy red water, not far from the bank, when he suddenly found himself caught in the current. As he struggled to regain his balance, the swift water pulled him away from the shoreline and a little ways out into a swirling eddy.

The dangerous river overpowered him. Struggle as he might, he couldn't keep his head above water. Though he remained in a relatively shallow spot, the force of the current had pushed him under into ominous darkness. He flailed around trying to kick, waving his arms, but nothing seemed to help. He felt he was suffocating.

Then it happened. Something inside him prompted him to stop fighting. He drifted downward a little more, then the strangest thing began to take place. He started to rise slowly toward the top, experiencing one of water's most magical properties: buoyancy. Though still submerged, he opened his eyes and peered upward. The river water was dark and murky, but Charles could barely make out a tiny speck of light directly above him. He remained still, not fighting the water, and in a few moments the top of his head cleared the surface. He immediately burst into fits of coughing, spitting, spewing water from his mouth.

As he jerked toward shore, he half-swam, half-drifted with frantic movements that looked more like a dog paddling or cat thrashing. Still gasping for breath, he dragged himself up on the muddy bank and lay there, exhausted, for several minutes.

When Charles realized he hadn't drowned during those terrifying moments, he turned and stared back at the river. For a long time, he just sat there reflecting on what he had just experienced.

"I guess you don't wanna keep this skinny Arkansas boy from the Bottoms," he whispered.

Over the next few years when no one was watching, Charles Jackson French would sneak away and walk the distance from the Bottoms down to the river, where he would slip in cautiously. Sometimes the water was calm and still, other times it flowed swiftly, even on occasion ferociously. He had come to realize how to "go with the flow" when the moment required. He practiced just being still and moving his hands around slowly at his sides. He learned that water would work with him if he did likewise. As he grew, his arms became stronger, his legs more coordinated.

The legendary Red River, though still dangerous, had birthed a friend . . . and one who could swim.

CHAPTER 2

Dangerous Waters, Part 2

"Your way was through the sea, your path through the great waters . . ." Psalm 77:19

Sailing in 1521 with five Spanish carracks, Ferdinand Magellan planned to circumnavigate the world. His ships had recently rounded South America, discovering the treacherous strait which today bears his name. They sailed on, ever westward. After weeks on the immense, endless waters of the Pacific Ocean, the voyagers finally landed at the southernmost isle of a vast 7,000-island territory. Magellan claimed it for Spain, and it was soon named in honor of Spain's prince and future king, Philip: the archipelago of the Philippines.

Unfortunately, a few short weeks later, the dauntless explorer was struck by a poison arrow. Magellan died before he could see one of the most magnificent bodies of water on earth still in its original, pristine condition—Manila Bay, the Pearl of the Orient, some 375 miles to the north.

Nearly landlocked, shimmering over 770 square miles with a 120-mile circumference, the harbor is spacious enough to divide into sections and deep enough—mostly thirty to fifty-five feet—to accommodate the largest vessel. Small islands are ideally positioned at its opening to support defensive weaponry, the islet of Corregidor proving particularly advantageous for this purpose.

Made for ships and sailors, traffic and trade, commerce and cargo, Manila Bay is favorably situated for routes traversing east or west, a natural crossroads in the South China Seas. The Bay's due west orientation creates memorable sunsets daily.

For men of the sea, it was a perfect harbor.

For eight-year-old Harry Bauer in 1911, it also seemed perfect but for completely different reasons.

Nearly every afternoon, he would walk with obvious pride along Roxas Boulevard, renamed Dewey Boulevard in honor of Commodore George Dewey, who defeated the Spanish fleet here in 1898. All up and down the waterfront promenade, rows and rows of massive coconut trees lined the rim of Manila Bay as far as one could see, a magnificent sight, particularly at sunset.

When Harry Bauer was a boy, he often walked along Roxas Boulevard in Manila, Philippines, with his father, Sgt. William Bauer, 7th Cavalry. Photo courtesy of Memories of Old Manila, Facebook page. Roxas Blvd. in 1914, Manila Bay.

But the reason for the boy's quick step didn't emanate from his surroundings—it was the persona of the man who strolled beside him: his father, Heinrich William Bauer, in uniform—the Sergeant Major for the 7th Cavalry with his wheeled field spurs clicking against his shiny knee-high boots, his long saber gleaming, his handlebar mustache freshly trimmed.

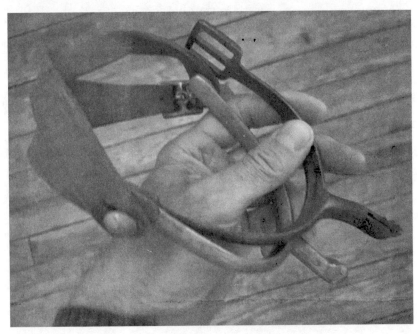

The original rowelled field spurs worn by Harry Bauer's father when the elder Bauer dressed in his 7th Cavalry uniform. Photo courtesy of Condra/Bauer family collection.

The Sergeant Major, who exuded an air of self-confidence, had signed on to tall ships as a cabin boy and had circumnavigated the world twice before he was fourteen years old. At eighteen, he had joined the US Army and had seen action in Cuba, the Spanish-American War, and later would participate in WWI for several months. Harry idolized him.

The Sergeant Major possessed a jovial, easygoing disposition, but one that could turn instantly stern if needed. He enjoyed his family and had brought them to the Philippines twice during deployments. His three children were born on or near army posts, with Harry being born on July 17, 1904, while his father was attached to the regimental camp near

Sgt. William Bauer, father of Harry Bauer, who followed in his dad's footsteps with a career in the military; Sgt. Bauer is shown here in his 7th Cavalry uniform. Photo courtesy of the Condra/Bauer family collection.

Lytle, Georgia, in the historic Chickamauga Park area across the river from Chattanooga, Tennessee.

Growing up in a military family, Harry naturally gravitated to ROTC at Chattanooga High School and became the school's Major. He served also as editor-in-chief of the yearbook, was a cheerleader, won the lead in several school plays, missed being elected Most Handsome and Most Popular by a mere handful of votes, and met his future wife, a beauty named Gladys Boyd, nicknamed "Jack." Once the pair became high school sweethearts, Harry's pet name for her was "Jackie."

Harry Bauer's Chattanooga High School yearbook, *Dynamo,* describes his character and personality in glowing terms of endearment: "A glorious record you have made at C.H.S. because you have put the best you have toward the interest of the school and we appreciate you and all you have done for us. Fifteen rahs for Bauer!"[*]

Similar accolades accompanied him in his freshman year at Chattanooga University:

> Born in Georgia, lived in the Philippines twice for luck, gave Kansas a treat for three or four years, took a whirl at Chattanooga, and then picked on us to finish his adolescence. In spite of all his wandering, however, he has the faculty of giving one the impression he is a model boy. In fact, he neither drinks, swears, nor chews, and is always turned in by ten P.M. If he had a single outstanding fault, it is his over-conscientiousness, which is considered by many as a virtue. He is eager to do the right thing by everybody. He is generous enough to lend his last dollar, and kindly forgetful enough not to ask for its return . . . we would emphatically state that we believe he will attain success and happiness.[†]

---

[*] High School yearbook, *The Dynamo*, Chattanooga High School, 1922.
[†] Chattanooga University yearbook, 1923.

In later life, the army junior would reminisce often about those afternoon strolls with his father around the Bay. The Bauers were a military family, one intrinsically connected to seas, waterways, bays, harbors: to water itself. He would never forget seeing Manila Bay calm and peaceful as he walked with his father . . . without warships, without guns booming, without men bolting to stations. However, he would always remember that his father had seen a completely different Manila Bay in the Spanish-American War and in years following.

As Harry grew older, he realized that water can be deceiving and perils can lie in calm harbors. Little did he know that one day Manila Bay would play a significant role in another major conflict, a worldwide conflict that would etch names like Bataan and Corregidor forever into his nation's conscience.

The beautiful Manila Bay had taught Harry one truth about water: dangers are often transported to calm waters, not by natural elements, but by people at war—and years later the conscientious young man would play a significant role in one of those wars.

CHAPTER 3

Preparing for Life, Preparing for War, Part 1

"Hear, O sons, a father's instruction, and be attentive, that you may gain insight . . ." Proverbs 4:1

Harry Bauer couldn't remember a time when he didn't want to attend the Naval Academy in Annapolis. The memory of his father standing straight and tall, dressed in his uniform and proud to be representing the United States, had made a lasting impression on his mind and heart. Added to those memories were world events during the last few years of the nineteenth century and the first two decades of the twentieth century, Harry's growing-up years. They brought personal introspection as well as focusing attention on the country's future well-being. In particular, interest in all things Navy had increased exponentially across the nation.

Like numerous movements in history, the surge often begins with a singular, massive event. When the USS *Maine* exploded and sank in Havana Harbor on a dark night in February 1898, it propelled the nation into war with Spain—no small matter. However, the limelight that subsequently descended on the Navy and its leader, Commodore George Dewey, was monumental.

To Dewey's fame and the Navy's glory, the gallant Commodore orchestrated a spectacular victory over the Spanish Fleet on May 1, 1898, catapulting both onto the world's stage. Victories spawn allocations. Just three days later, Congress appropriated $1 million for a complete overhaul of the Naval Academy, including a new armory, boathouse, and powerhouse, among other buildings. Two years later, another $8 million was designated for additional structures. Noted architect Ernest Flagg, who had studied at the Ecole des Beaux-Arts in Paris, was tapped to spearhead the project. Under his immense design genius, Flagg drafted some of the most stunning buildings on any campus in the nation.*

Not only did the country as a whole sharpen its interest in the Navy, but the number of young men seeking admission to the Naval Academy escalated. Those from military families, particularly those whose fathers were or had been enlisted, seemed especially motivated. Through the 1920s and '30s, a sense of urgency permeated the activities of all military academies. Many factors contributed to this, but primarily World War I brought a sobering reality to all nations. Then, a brief decade later, the Great Depression brought another kind of sobering reality: How do I feed myself and my family? When local jobs proved too hard to find, joining the military often became the only option.

To gain entrance into the Naval Academy, an applicant needed a sponsor; procuring one sometimes took longer than expected. So, after Harry graduated from high school, he first enrolled at Chattanooga University while actively seeking a recommendation. When attorney and congressman Joe Brown read Harry's resume, he arranged to meet him personally. He immediately initiated the necessary procedures and gladly represented the amiable, impressive young man who had grown up loving to walk beside his soldier-father laced with saber and spurs.

In 1923 Harry entered the Naval Academy at Annapolis and, just as he had done in high school, made friends quickly with everyone. The Academy's yearbook *The Lucky Bag*, known as the largest yearbook in the world, heaped accolades on the conscientious young man:

> Though one of the prime members of the bridge and poker clubs, we can see at a glance that he is one of those nearly extinct individuals who believe that life will return him

---

* history.navy.mil ("The United States Naval Academy, 1845–2020," by Jim Cleevers, edited by Sharon Kennedy, U.S. Naval Academy).

measure for measure, and we would emphatically state that we believe he will attain success and happiness.*

Throughout his time at the Academy, Harry stayed in close touch with his high school sweetheart, Gladys "Jackie" Boyd. Following graduation in 1927, while serving in shore assignments, Harry and Jackie decided it was time to tie the knot. There really had never been any question about where their relationship would eventually end up. They had worked on their high school yearbook staff together, participated in many of the same Chattanooga High School activities, and were always seen together walking hand in hand.

While Harry was at the Academy, Jackie enjoyed visiting Annapolis often for ceremonies and balls. And in 1929 the pretty Tennessee girl became a Navy wife who thought her husband's dress whites only added to his good looks.

In another year or so, Harry applied for postgraduate work at the Academy and received acceptance as well as an instructor's position. The next three years were a wonderful season for the couple. The two seemed made for each other, a couple with cordial manners and liked by all. While Harry was still instructing at the Academy, they were blessed with a daughter in 1935 and named her Emilie Geyer. But Harry, who doted over his sweet baby girl, quickly began calling her "Mimi," a pet name that stuck throughout her life.

These were lovely days together, a welcome reprieve from the oppressive days of the Great Depression. Though the Navy had experienced the weight of trying financial times, as did the entire country, Harry and Jackie felt blessed to have a home and friends within the military community. Among their many friends was a classmate named Edward M. Condra, also from a military family. Ed was a star on the football team and captain of the baseball team. Their friendship deepened when Harry

---

* *The Lucky Bag*, 1927, Naval Academy, Harry F. Bauer, Class of '27, usnamem orialhall.org.

introduced Ed to his sister, Martha Lois. The two hit it off and eventually married, making Harry and Ed brothers-in-law. Both would play key roles in the looming war.

Another close friend of the Bauers was Gus Lofberg Jr., a classmate from Racine, Wisconsin, son of Lt. Gus Lofberg Sr., who was in charge of the local Coast Guard station from 1903 to 1914. Gus, sometimes called "Swede," returned to instruct at the Academy at the same time Harry returned to pursue a postgraduate degree while instructing. They had both married by this time and in 1935 shared another life experience—they both became parents of a daughter. It would, however, not be the final shared experience of their lives.

After instructing at the Academy for about three years, Harry was to experience firsthand knowledge of sea duty from assignments on three very interesting and very different ships. The young seaman loved every minute of it. He began to understand personally the popular declaration that there exists a "love affair between men and ships"—although he would always laugh and say there was only one true love of his life, and she was back home taking care of the baby.

His first sea duty was on the USS *Twiggs*, a Wickes-class destroyer laid down on January 23, 1918, during WWI and named after Marine Major Levi Twiggs. The Major was killed during the Battle of Chapultepec in Mexico in 1847; 90 percent of the Marines in that battle were killed. In their honor, according to Marine Corps history, a solid scarlet stripe or "blood" stripe is worn down the outside seam of their blue trousers. In later years, this battle inspired the first line of the well-known "Marines' Hymn," "From the halls of Montezuma . . ." After several different escort duties, the USS *Twiggs* was one of fifty ships transferred to the British in exchange for 99-year leases on strategic base sites in the Western Hemisphere. Years later, while still with the British, the aging "old girl" gained a unique celebrity status as the HMS *Ballantrae* on the big screen in 1952 when she was featured in a British film starring Trevor Howard and Richard Attenborough titled *The Gift Horse*. It was an immediate hit among moviegoers.

After spending time on the *Twiggs*, Harry was transferred to the USS *Cuyama*, a tanker named after the Cuyama River in Southern California that begins at 8,000 feet above sea level in the Chumash Wilderness. The tanker was utilized as the first test ship in developing "alongside" refueling, a major factor in success of the naval war against Japan. It allowed ships to continue running at near full speed rather than slowing or stopping to refuel. The young officer learned the technique firsthand, a skill that would serve him well in coming years.

Next, Harry did duty on the USS *Tracy*, a Clemson-class destroyer and the only US ship ever named for a Secretary of the Navy, Benjamin Franklin Tracy.[*]

In each instance, these ships reinforced Harry Bauer's love of the sea, love of ships, love for the Navy. And he was an avid reader of history, especially Navy history, and the naming of ships fascinated him.

Each ship, because of Navy protocol, carried a bit of history—or some other important aspect inherent in the United States of America—and celebrated it. Aircraft carriers were often named after presidents, battleships for states, cruisers for famous battles, and destroyers for noted service members in the navy or Marines. There were notable exceptions in each category, but each ship kept alive the memory of some notable place, thing or person. He dreamed and prayed for the day when he might have a ship under his own command, but first there would need to be promotions.[†]

It wasn't long, however, before part of his lifelong dream began to take shape. By the late 1930s, the world's march towards war seemed more inevitable with each passing day. On July 1, 1941, just sixteen days before his thirty-seventh birthday, Harry Frederick Bauer was commissioned Lieutenant Commander in the United Sates Navy.

---

[*]   Wikipedia—https://en.wikipedia.org.wiki.USS_Tracy.
[†]   See "Appendix A: Reference for Ship Naming in the USN."

LIEUT. COMDR.. , U.S.N.

Harry F. Bauer, Lieutenant Commander, given command of the USS *Gregory* on January 1, 1942. Photo courtesy of Navy Military Archives (Golden Arrow Research).

CHAPTER 3

Preparing for Life, Preparing for War, Part 2

*"Father of the fatherless . . . is God in His holy habitation.
God settles the solitary in a home . . ." Psalm 68:5–6*

Foreman wasn't always the name of Charles Jackson French's birth-place. In the early 1800s, Native Americans, mainly Cherokees and Choctaws, called the area Willow Springs because of the numerous wispy trees creating cool shade throughout the natural springs. When they noticed wild animals getting drinks of water around the edges lined with large rocks, then resting under the willows, they began calling it Rocky Comfort. Eventually, a small but thriving town sprang up on flatter land nearby.

After the Arkansas and Choctaw Railroad laid track through the virgin forests one mile from Rocky Comfort in 1895, businessmen, growers, and local residents recognized the potential of living even closer to the railroad. Soon after building on both sides of the track, a second community began to flourish and residents dubbed their town New Rocky Comfort.

However, when the US Postal Service was established in 1900, a problem ensued: the name "New Rocky Comfort" was too lengthy and cumbersome for swift transactions, aesthetic descriptions aside. Before long, they selected the name "Foreman" for the town in honor of Ben Foreman, a prominent civic leader from Texarkana. Some wheels turn slowly, however, and the new name was not legally adopted until 1959.

For several decades cotton had been the main industry of Little River County with its collection of small towns and communities. The Depression brought severe suffering, much like in the rest of the country. Farmers had to sell their farms, wages plummeted, and unemployment exploded. Wages dropped one-third after 1929. Everyone was searching for work.

Foreman, Arkansas, in the early 1900s, the town next to the Bottomland of the Red River where Charles Jackson French was born and reared. Photo courtesy of William B. Harp, Mayor of Foreman, AK.

Charles's father, Jackson French, picked cotton, completed odd jobs, baled hay, literally anything to make a living during the Depression years. Food was scarce everywhere, and Charles often watched his mother cut up a couple of potatoes to brown in an iron skillet on a makeshift wood stove in their crude sharecropper's cabin for supper. Sometimes, she would allow the eager boy to help, especially if there was an egg or two to cook along with the spuds.

One day in spring 1930, ten-year-old Charles was late walking home from school. The teacher had kept him after class for talking; his punishment was to write "I will not talk in class" twenty-five times on the small blackboard behind her desk. It was not the first time Charles had been detained, since the energetic boy found it difficult to sit still without interacting with those around him. His slight frame made him an easy target for jokes and teasing, but Charles never allowed his size to deter him. He was scrappy and almost never backed down—unless, of course, he could turn it to his advantage.

On this warm afternoon, he felt relieved the writing punishment was over and enjoyed the feel of warm grass on his bare feet. As he rounded the last curve in the path that led to his home, he looked up to see his mother kneeling in the dirt at the porch step. Charles couldn't see exactly what she was draped over, but as he approached, he recognized the scruffy work shoes and dusty pant legs of his father's overalls.

Charles just stood there for a moment. Finally, his mother looked up and blankly stared at him.

"Your daddy, he's dead," she said. "Go fetch Chester and Viola." There was no expression on his mother's face or in her voice, simply resignation.

In the weeks and months following, neighbors, relatives, and members from their local church did what they could to help out Louisa and her children, but everyone was struggling. The Depression years took their toll. A year later, while Charles and his brother and sisters slept, their mother passed away in the night. Charles spent most of that following day fighting the currents in the Red River.

Within two years, both of Charles's older sisters left home. He himself made up his mind that he would join the Navy as soon as he could. Others in his situation were also doing the same—they knew they would be paid, fed, and supplied with clothes.

So, in late 1937, two months after his eighteenth birthday, he decided to enlist. His older brother, Chester French, helped fill out his application, signing as nearest relative. Character references on his application form included Dr. Casteel, who had a small medical office in downtown Foreman for seeing patients, though he made house calls as well; Jim Elliott and J. E. Cannon, who were local farmers; and Fred Gant, who owned a mercantile store.

On December 4, 1937, five-foot-six Charles Jackson French, weighing in at 128 pounds, was accepted into the Navy as a Mess Attendant 3rd Class, one of the few jobs open to African Americans at that time in the Navy. Within a couple of weeks, he reported in for his initial naval training in Norfolk, Virginia. There were many things the teenager from rural Arkansas, who had never been far from home, had to learn.

But much to the surprise of his instructors, swimming was not one of them.

Enlistment photo of Charles Jackson French for his first period in the Navy, December 4, 1937, five feet six, 128 lb. Photo courtesy of Navy Military Archives (Golden Arrow Research).

CHAPTER 4

Blue Water

"Thus says the LORD, who gives the sun for light by day and the fixed order of the moon and the stars for light by night, who stirs up the sea so that its waves roar—the LORD of hosts is his name." Jeremiah 31:35

Charles arrived in Norfolk, Virginia, for basic training in December 1937. Like many teenagers growing up in the Depression era, unless a family possessed military ties or flourished financially, there was a fair chance travel had been limited. Charles's introduction to Navy life included a host of different experiences, none more breathtaking than a singularly arresting moment, in reality an epiphany: it was the first time the youth from landlocked Arkansas had ever seen the ocean.

His first view of the Atlantic occurred shortly after arriving on base. Stout curling waves, hypnotic sounds, sea birds, and beaches—all were mesmerizing. However, the explosion of light at daybreak over water that seemed to go forever made the most distinct impression. It would be a spectacle Charles never tired of seeing.

Once on board ship, watching the sun rise over "Blue Water" would become a favorite pastime when he could sneak a few moments out on deck during early morning hours. He had never heard the term Blue Water. It refers to the global deep oceans, the open seas. And a Blue Water Navy, like the United States Navy, is a true example of the term—meaning the United States has a navy whose fleets have successfully spanned across the deep waters of the open oceans of the globe.

By the end of his second tour in the Navy in 1944, Charles Jackson French had traversed back and forth across the Pacific twice, navigating the Coral Sea, the South China Seas, the Bismarck Sea while sailing over 40,000 miles in Blue Water. Yet, there would be one body of water Charles Jackson French would never forget—*could* never forget, neither in his waking hours or sleeping—a body of water in the depths of the South Pacific, deceptive in daylight, transformational at night.

But that was still a few years away in the future.

For now, the three months of training in Norfolk kept the new mess attendant absorbed with standard entrance components of "a swimming test, physical fitness training sessions, marching, weapons training and a few classroom courses . . . subjects including U.S. Navy history, Navy uniforms and commands, Navy ships and aircraft, first aid, and conduct during Navy missions."[*]

Norfolk introduced him to all things Navy. He was issued uniforms and was cut his first monthly paycheck of $36. In some ways, it seemed like the Christmas he never knew—lots of new clothes, new shoes, a new wool peacoat, all just handed to him. And he was fed three squares a day . . . always with dessert—which he never skipped. The skinny young man began gaining weight.

Charles took the rigorous schedule in stride. He had grown up accustomed to people rising early and working hard through daylight hours; starting when you could see, stopping when you couldn't. His first actual introduction to ships came on the USS *Antares*, a cargo ship acquired by the Navy after WWI and named for the brightest star in the constellation, Scorpius.

After boarding, he could hardly believe how massive she was. The vessel, which at the time operated with the Training Detachment, could handle heavy Marine equipment, including the experimental tank lighter and artillery lighter, used for amphibious landings on hostile shores.

Here in the belly of *Antares,* Charles learned firsthand the duties of a mess attendant. These consisted of serving three "squares" a day to a

---

[*] history.navy.mil, *The Wardroom*, NavPers10002-A, 1.

crew of seventeen officers and 213 enlisted, which was approximately 700 meals every twenty-four hours. This required constant and consistent cleaning round-the-clock, mopping, sweeping, dusting, wiping down surfaces—the goal being to keep the mess from becoming a mess. Dishes, glasses, and cutlery were all washed with care to avoid breakage. Charles learned that lesson quickly, as any broken dinnerware resulted in docked pay of the transgressor.

Mostly each day had its preset meal, meaning that on Monday there was a certain menu that was then repeated every Monday. Tuesday had its menu, and so forth—year after year. Sailors could actually look at their plate of food and know what day it was, which often proved beneficial. On some ADPs, the Saturday/Wednesday morning breakfast beans were accompanied by cornbread and bowls of "red lead," sailors' nickname for catsup.

However, on any holiday, such as July Fourth or Christmas, the cooks and mess attendants served a feast with all the trimmings. These holiday menus varied from holiday to holiday; cooks and mess deck attendants did their best to be creative.

For example, here is a sample Fourth of July menu (as it was printed) from one APD in 1941:

Menu
July 4, 1941

Stuffed Tomatoes

Sweet Pickles   Celery Hearts

Cream of Tomato Soup

Crackers

Fried Chicken   Giblet Gravy

Mashed Potatoes

Creamed Peas and Carrots

Avocado Salad

Hot Rolls   Butter

Lemonade

Cake and Ice Cream

Coffee

Cigars   Cigarettes

After three months of initial training on the *Antares*, Mess Attendant French was given an assignment for regular duty. During his first four-year enlistment period, the young sailor would spend more than half of his time at sea on two ships, the USS *Louisville* and the USS *Houston*, serving sixteen months and thirteen months respectively.

The *Louisville*, a heavy cruiser with a crew of 621 men, was considerably larger than the *Antares* and operated primarily off the west coast. The mess attendants, numbering around twenty-five, were hardworking—always cleaning, preparing, serving, then cleaning again for over 1,800 meals per day. In 1938, she began a long Pacific cruise that took her to Hawaii, Samoa, Australia, and Tahiti. The teenager from Arkansas, who had seldom ventured out of his home county, was off to see the world.

Like most novice sailors plunging through Blue Water on their first voyage, a significant portion of time was spent hanging over the rails. But it didn't take Charles long to acquire sea legs. He adapted quickly and easily to ocean sailing and enjoyed the busy schedule; even the tight quarters didn't bother him. But, like all men on ships, he eagerly anticipated times when he could be on deck; there were always different cloud formations, a kaleidoscope of variegated colors, skies, the ocean itself continually morphing whether daytime or nighttime.

After nearly two weeks, the *Louisville* arrived at her destination; the exotic beauty of the Hawaiian Islands presented as soon as the ship cruised into Pearl. Sweet, citrusy air was permeated with aromas of pineapple, plumeria, and pikake, a profusely fragrant white flower from the jasmine family that's beloved for its beauty and sweet scent. Shore leave offered an endless array of things to do, and the narrow streets were jammed with men in uniform. Dark, long-haired beauties sashayed everywhere. Cheap booze was easy to find, as was warm beer at the Pearl City Tavern where monkeys scampered atop the bar holding out their tin begging cups. Sailors quickly discovered the monkeys had learned something too—to topple over the drinks of chintzy revelers who didn't share their coins with the mischievous primates.

Charles, like so many sailors, had no problem acquiring a taste for ropy liquor, nor was the beauty of native girls lost on him. Feisty, full of fun, with a broad smile set in a handsome face, the nineteen-year-old soon gained mutual acceptance among the islanders.

On October 28, 1939, after nearly a year and a half on the *Louisville*, Charles transferred to the USS *Houston*, another heavy cruiser that later received the honor of flagship for the Asiatic Fleet. (This honor signifies a ship that carries the commander of a fleet and flies the commander's flag.) During the first couple of months, Charles acclimated to a new ship and new peers in the mess; he also encountered something else new—confinement in the brig for three days on bread and water. His offense was recorded on the Mast Report Slip: "Using improper language in the Wardroom Pantry; while sitting in The Wardroom, I heard the mess attendants in the pantry argue in a loud voice and use the following words: 'Fuck' and 'Shit.' Mahew was with French." The Mast Report Slip was signed and witnessed by two lieutenants.

The Navy, especially in the 1920s and '30s, was well known for its strict decorum and adherence to "the rules." A famous movie about WWII has one character, an Air Force pilot, urging his girlfriend to leave with him immediately from a Navy country club saying, "C'mon baby, let's get out of this stuffy Navy joint."

All protocol was expected to be smartly adhered to both on ship and off. This adherence to a gentleman's Code of Conduct has roots centuries old. John Paul Jones declared in September 1775:

> "It is by no means enough that an officer of the navy should
> be a capable mariner. He must be that of course, but also a
> great deal more. He should be as well a gentleman of liberal
> education, refined manners, punctilious courtesy, and the
> nicest sense of personal honor."

An official naval pamphlet titled "In the Wardroom," published by the Bureau of Naval Personnel, outlines all the various codes of conduct expected by active-duty members. Article #9 of the fundamental dictates to be avoided in naval protocol is: "Any kind of cheap, vulgar, uncultivated talk, especially to or in the presence of an enlisted man." It goes without saying that these fundamental dictates were to be respected and followed by enlisted sailors as well. Nowhere aboard ship were strict rules more proudly maintained than in the Wardroom.

This pamphlet was first prepared as a guide for officers of the Amphibious Force, US Atlantic Fleet. In promulgating it, Vice Admiral F. G. Fahrion stated:

"The important purpose of this pamphlet is to furnish the command of this Force, including every officer in our wardrooms, with a background of information pertinent to establishing and maintaining the highest standards in the 'wardrooms' of the Amphibious Force, U. S. Atlantic Fleet. Since this objective is a highly worthy one in all wardrooms, the pamphlet is being reprinted for the use of all newly commissioned and junior officers of the Navy. Its use should assist materially in furnishing that background of information pertinent to establishing and maintaining the highest standards in the wardrooms of the Fleet."[*]

It would not be the last time Charles received a few days in the brig. The following year he got into a fight with another sailor, and for this offense, he endured five days of "bread and water" in the brig. Over-indulgence in alcohol became an issue as well, since sailors were not allowed to have liquor aboard ship.

The offenses added up. When it came time for him to leave the Navy on November 19, 1941, his paperwork listed him as "Not recommended for re-enlistment."

What a difference a brief eighteen days would make.

---

[*] history.navy.mil, *The Wardroom*, NavPers, 1–2.

CHAPTER 5

Memories: December 7, 1992

". . . And in Your Book were all written, every one of them, the days that were formed for me . . ." Psalm 139:16

B ob Adrian bent over and placed the small tin bowl of leftover scrambled eggs on the back stoop. Bushy Tail awaited eagerly; the large cat's bright orange fur puffed out against the frigid air.

"There you go," said Bob, who never failed to lay out scraps for neighborhood strays. "Cold out here today. You stay out of trouble, Bushy Tail." The cat looked up appreciatively as Bob shut the basement door.

Pulling his jacket tighter around his neck, he strode down the dark corridor toward his command center office. The temperature had hovered around 36° with a 20-mph wind all morning. He switched on the floor heater and settled in at his desk. A small flip calendar stared at him: December 7, 1992. Fifty-one years had passed, yet it seemed like yesterday.

Bob stared back at the calendar. "Of course, the whole world for us changed on December 7, 1941, when the Japanese attacked Pearl Harbor," he thought. Like every American alive on that day, he could recall exactly where he was and what he was doing when he heard the news.

"Earl Tuhy, one of my classmates, and I were out seeing a movie, at the time of the attack, and when we returned to the Academy, the whole war started there. They graduated the Class of '41, and sent them off to war in about two weeks; then they scheduled the Class of '42 to graduate in April; and then, just two months later, our Class of '43 moved up to graduate that June 1942—one full year ahead of schedule. In our academics, it seemed like we went through one book a week and had classes Monday through Saturday, and two days off that Christmas." *

He remembered how he and Joan had made plans to be married in the Naval Academy Chapel after graduation with both of their parents there for the graduation ceremony, then the marriage ceremony. However, Joan's mom was not well at the time. Since he had fifteen days before he had to report in San Francisco for "shipping out," they decided to wait until they returned to their hometown to tie the knot.

But they did manage to squeeze in one last memory to celebrate Navy Academy graduation: they spent the weekend with a few friends in New York City. The trip was topped off by a wonderful evening at the Astor Roof to hear Tommy Dorsey playing for Frank Sinatra and the Pied Pipers—all Bob's favorites. He could still hear Sinatra crooning the hit song, "Once in a While."

"What a swell time that was, singing and dancing with my gal. And what a love story we've had," he thought, grinning out loud.

Ahh, Joan. Pronounced Jo-Ann, she was five-foot-two, eyes of sparkling brown, and a real firecracker. Loved to sing, hum, whistle, and filled a room with sunshine as soon as she entered. Though they never lived next door, Bob Adrian and Joan Smith had known each other since grade school. They played and skated together, were members of the same school clubs, starred opposite each other in plays, and had been best friends from the first day they met: but always just friends—nothing else. Never had a date together. Each had other romantic interests along the way, one girl, in particular, for Bob.

As the young man was considering the possibility of seeking an appointment to the Naval Academy, his then girlfriend called and said she wanted to meet to discuss their "future relationship."

---

* Robert Adrian, memoirs.

Ensign Robert Nelson Adrian, Class of '43. The class actually had an accelerated graduation due to the onset of war in the Pacific. This picture was taken of Bob Adrian in June 1942 as his graduation photo. Photo courtesy of the Adrian Family Collection.

Bob recalled vividly what happened that night. He had met her for dinner. "I told her that I had taken the exam for entrance to the Naval Academy, and hoped I would make it for the four years there. She responded that she wasn't going to wait for me that long, so I paid the dinner check and said 'Good-bye-Good luck' and left her sitting there."*

After Bob's plebe year at the Academy and completing a two-month battleship practice squadron cruise to South America, he returned to his

---

* Ibid.

home in Ontario, Oregon, a small village on the Snake River border of Idaho. He relished the thought of an entire month of leave during August—to catch up with family and friends. A chance encounter with his bestie of many years was about to develop into something entirely different.

"On my first day of leave, and dressed in my white summer uniform—we were encouraged to wear our uniform at all times when in public, and civilian wear only when in recreational activities—I walked down Main St. and was welcomed home by many of my acquaintances. I then went into the bank where I saw Joan Smith sitting at the Secretary's desk outside the Bank Manager's Office. And 'Bang—It Was Love At First Sight!' I hadn't seen her for two years while she finished her business school in Portland and returned to Ontario and got this prime job.

"I asked her if she was dating and she said 'No, not at this time.' So I asked her for a date that evening, and she accepted. It would be our first date after knowing one another for most of our lives.

"When I left the bank, I said to myself, that after so many years of knowing and admiring Joan, WHY had I not fallen in love with her before?!"*

The couple knew almost immediately they wished to spend the rest of their lives together—why not? They had spent most of their growing-up years together. Joan and Bob made plans to get married as soon as possible. Little could they know how one Sunday morning in Hawaii would change everything.

"Yes," thought Robert Nelson Adrian in his cold basement wardroom, "December 7, 1941, was quite a day. I had no idea what would happen, what ship I'd be on, where I would be going, or the people I would meet and never forget. It certainly ushered in a different era for all of us—yet one I wouldn't give anything in the world for having lived through."

A distant meowing abruptly broke into his meditations. "Guess Bushy Tail's hungry again," he said to himself, and headed towards the basement galley to round up some more rations for his feline friend.

---

* Ibid.

CHAPTER 6

Day of Infamy: December 7, 1941

"When the earth totters, and all its inhabitants, it is I who keep steady its pillars." Psalm 75:3

Gathered around radios in living rooms across the country and intercom loudspeakers on ships and military bases, Americans listened attentively to the eloquent, mellow voice announcing the unthinkable. The world was at war. "No matter how long it takes us to overcome this premeditated invasion, the American people in their righteous might will win . . . through to absolute victory," said President Franklin Delano Roosevelt.

James Bassett, in his classic WWII novel titled *Harm's Way*, depicts a commander on a ship out of Pearl Harbor. Bassett was ideally suited to write about these events since in real life, he was in the Navy and stationed at Pearl Harbor during the attack. Later, he became the public relations officer for Admiral "Bull" Halsey.

In the movie version of Bassett's bestseller, after realizing that a state of war now officially existed, a lieutenant commander exclaims to his captain, "Ohhh, Rock of ages, we've got ourselves another war—a gut-busting, mother-lovin' Navy war!" It's probably not out of the realm of possibility that some sailor somewhere voiced something similar in real time. Others were actually heard to shout out expletives and various versions of "Now we can kill Japs legal!"

For professional military, purgatory is one of two scenarios: a desk job or the winds of war without being at war—*officially*. Once the bombing of Pearl Harbor occurred on the morning of December 7, 1941, both scenarios became obsolete. Men were taken from desk jobs and plugged into more active positions where needed. And men in potentially active combat sections could now carry out what they were trained to do—"kill and blow up things."

In the first few hours after the bombing, orders were already being transmitted to units across the globe, especially to Navy commanders: "Seek out and engage the enemy—Godspeed" was the cryptic message of the day. Though at some level regret may have accompanied this situation, there existed no thought of backing down.

America was woefully ill-prepared for a two-front war. But it was not for lack of courage or will. By the afternoon of December 7, 1941, thousands of young men had abandoned their "Easy-Like-Sunday-Morning" and raced to the nearest recruiting office. Twenty-one-year-old Archie Rackerby, who later became a Marine Raider in 3rd Raider Battalion, said by the time he drove from his home in Sacramento and arrived at the military depot in San Francisco that afternoon, double lines of applicants stretched for blocks in every direction.

As the days rolled on, reports continually surfaced of young men who were informed they had flunked their physical and therefore couldn't join up. Many who weren't able to fight for their country took their own lives in despair. What was lacking in preparedness was made up in resolve: an overwhelming willingness to defend a beloved homeland.

Sunday, December 7, 1941, was just another Lord's Sabbath at "the Yard," the colloquial nickname for the Naval Academy campus: early morning chapel, touring visitors, and clean-up detail after a Saturday night "hop" at Smoke Hall, the magnificent lower portion of Bancroft Hall, open only to midshipmen activities.

But by midafternoon, as word of the attack circulated, the entire campus buzzed. Visitors were hastened out the gates by guards, the waterfront quickly secured with small craft. Before long, blackout blinds shielded windows and lower floors of buildings designated as potential raid shelters. As one midshipman exclaimed afterwards, "The Academy went wild with excitement!"

Immediately, all aspects of military training at the Yard accelerated to produce quality officer material for a two-ocean war. Academy grads formed the professional core, around which the Navy's unprecedented expansion from 119,088 uniformed personnel in 1938 to 3,405,525 in 1945 could occur. Nearly all of the war's key naval leaders were graduates: Ernest King, Class of '01; William Halsey, '04; Chester Nimitz, '05; and Raymond Spruance, '06. Altogether, alumni from fifty-four classes participated in the war. Between 1941 and 1945, the Academy contributed more than 7,500 officers to the fleet.

Harry Bauer would have been part of that "wild excitement" at the Yard, had he still been part of the faculty. But after teaching a couple of years, then serving another tour at sea, he had been transferred to the only place on the planet where the "excitement" could match and, in fact, surpass what was occurring at the Academy on that Sunday afternoon. In February 1939, he had been assigned to the Office of Detail Officer at the Bureau of Navigation, Department of the Navy, Washington, DC—for all practical purposes, Navy Headquarters.

The Bureau of Navigation had a long history, dating back to its inception in 1862. This large division was responsible for naval personnel management, including all paperwork and records, all nautical charts, maps, and instruments. In 1941, partly because of growing numbers of service members, its responsibilities narrowed to primarily personnel management.

Just three months after Bauer arrived at the hub of all things Navy, Chester W. Nimitz was named Chief of the Bureau. Then just a couple of months after the arrival of Nimitz, Harry was promoted to Lt. Commander.

Harry liked the unflappable Nimitz immediately. Both were of German heritage and had been deeply influenced by military family members; Harry by his father and Nimitz by his paternal grandfather, who had been a former seaman with the German Merchant Marine. Nimitz would remember for a lifetime what his grandfather had said of the sea—that "life itself was like the sea, a stern taskmaster. The best way to get along with either is to learn all you can, then do your best and don't worry—especially about things over which you have no control."[*]

Bauer thrived in the environment. His charming ability to get along with everyone served him well, and his natural gift of organization and administrative skills were commensurate with his position. Along with his wife, he immensely enjoyed the opportunities for socializing with other officers and their spouses; Washington provided an endless pot-pourri of things to do for the Bauers.

On December 7, 1941, Harry and Jackie Bauer returned home from early church services at Covenant-First Presbyterian Church and finished a light Sunday brunch instead of their usual, more formal Sunday dinner at noon. Their six-year-old daughter, Mimi, looked forward with special excitement to an afternoon of family festivities. Her parents had promised she could help decorate the Christmas tree her dad had brought home the day before. There would be homemade cookies to nibble and small candy canes to dangle from tree limbs. Later in the day, some friends were scheduled to come over for Sunday night supper.

The last of the tree lights were being threaded in the branches, Jackie directing Harry with a few adjustments at the top of the tree. Mimi was already playing around the lower limbs when the phone rang. Harry went to the kitchen and answered it. After a pause, he shouted, "What? Oh no—I'm on my way!"

Jackie couldn't imagine what was so alarming. She started to ask her husband when he reappeared, but one look at his face stopped her short. He simply said, "The Japanese have attacked Pearl Harbor!" He immediately called for a military car to come for him and hastily left for the Navy Department in downtown Washington, DC By the time he arrived at the large seven-story building, there were cars pulling up with Navy

---

[*]   The American Presidency Project: Remarks at the USS *Nimitz* Commissioning Ceremony in Norfolk Virginia by President Gerald Ford, May 3, 1975; www .presidency.ucsb.edu.

officers quickly emerging, one after another, and hurrying into the building.

Before this news reached the White House, President Roosevelt had only one appointment on his calendar scheduled for that Sunday: a 12:30 p.m. meeting with the Chinese ambassador. Now, his personal secretary, Grace Tully, worked frantically to schedule appointments, filling the remainder of the president's day through midnight: advisors, cabinet members, congressional leaders, all dropped what they were doing to confer with the president about the national crisis. At midnight, according to Tully's handwritten schedule, "Mr. Ed Murrow and Col. William J. Donovan" met with the president, thus closing the Day of Days . . . but just opening the long season of World War.*

---

* Edward R. Murrow, influential radio broadcaster who helped shape public opinion in America during the pre-war years and beyond; Col. William "Wild Bill" J. Donovan, soldier, lawyer, diplomat, is considered the founding father of the CIA.

CHAPTER 7

Signing Up . . . Again

". . . though war rise against me, I will be confident." Psalm 27:3

The news of the bombing of Pearl Harbor jarred Charles Jackson French. Two of the ships he had served on were at Pearl that morning. Many crew members he had known—friends of his—remained aboard both ships, and he hoped they were okay.

When he was discharged from the Navy, Charles joined his older sister, Viola French, in Omaha. She had moved there from Foreman seeking better employment opportunities. With war on the horizon, some factories and supply businesses had begun increasing their workforce.

In 1940, the US Army Air Corps selected Offutt Field just south of Omaha as the site for new bomber production. The enormous thirty-nine-acre aircraft assembly plant, a two-mile-long runway, and six large hangars opened in January 1942. The plant immediately began producing nearly 1,600 B-26 Marauders, then later switched to producing the B-29 Superfortresses, including the *Enola Gay*, personally selected by Paul Tibbets from the assembly line. The plant was operated by the Glen L. Martin Company.

As war became official, men were pulled off assembly lines and women sought to replace them. Viola, a small, energetic young woman, immediately applied for a position and was accepted. Her salary more than doubled any she had ever earned before. Like so many of the women applicants, being country raised meant limited if any exposure to machinery other than the essentials: plows and pumps. However, with workshops provided at the plant on manufacturing and basic industrial skills, she quickly learned what was necessary to be a reliable operator on the assembly lines. At the Martin plant in Nebraska, nearly 40 percent of the plant's employees during the war were women, making it one of the largest recruiters of women war workers. The female work force across the country took great pride in their contributions to the war effort, motivated by patriotism and the desire to help assist their families with higher wages.

Viola had adequate income to rent a small second-floor apartment in a private house on North Twenty-Fifth Street. At one end of the main room was a small kitchenette and down the hall, a common bath. When Charles got out of the Navy, he rode the bus to Omaha and was welcomed by Viola to share her apartment. He was there less than three weeks before announcing he planned to rejoin the Navy.

"Charles, you sure that's what you wanna do?" Viola raised her eyebrows, somewhat surprised her brother would want to turn around and get right back in. "How do you know they'll even take you?"

"Oh, they'll take me back," her brother said, "they need men. Besides, I *wanna* get back in. I had buddies who were at Pearl. Heck, *I* could've been there. Our enemy needs a whuppin."

French had learned that the USS *New Orleans*, the heavy cruiser he had been stationed on for Anti-Aircraft and Broadside Gunnery School, was docked for engine repair in Pearl Harbor on December 7, 1941. When the dock and yard power failed under the attack, engineers on board worked feverishly with flashlights to raise enough steam to get her moving. Until then, she was a ripe target for the waves of Zeroes flying over. Sailors on deck were reduced to using rifles and pistols to shoot at enemy aircraft—bullets, bombs, and shrapnel creating fiery chaos everywhere. Many were badly injured during the melee.

In the pandemonium, keys to ammo boxes couldn't be located and the big five-inch/25-caliber AA gun had to be operated manually. Without power, the ammunition hoists didn't function—the fifty-four-pound shells had to be hoisted by hand using ropes.

Mess attendants without a specific job went topside to help form long serpentine ammunition lines to help relay ammo from below. Many were severely injured when a fragmentation bomb exploded on deck. During the attack, the ship's chaplain who French remembered as a "good guy," Howell Forgy, walked up and down the lines encouraging sailors amidst flying bullets and explosions with admonitions of "Praise the Lord and pass the ammunition!"

Not only was the *New Orleans* docked there, but the very first ship Charles ever set foot on, training ship USS *Antares,* was just off the entrance to Pearl Harbor at 6:30 a.m. that Sunday morning, December 7, 1941. She had recently arrived from Canton and Palmyra islands with a 500-ton steel barge in tow. A tug was supposed to meet her at the entrance and take the tow, then the *Antares* was scheduled to enter Pearl Harbor itself.

But the tug didn't show. As the *Antares* slowly steered eastward to await the tug, a suspicious object was spotted about 1,500 yards to starboard. The object appeared like what might be the upper portion of a submarine conning tower with periscope up. Though it couldn't be positively identified, the *Antares*'s captain alerted shore patrol and the vessel *Ward* sped to the site. Once there, the patrol ship commenced firing while a patrol plane dropped bombs. The *Ward* also dropped three depth charges over the object which disappeared.

By this time, explosions all over Pearl Harbor could be clearly observed from the *Antares*. As a training ship she was not armed and completely vulnerable to an attack. Without further delay, the captain requested to enter Honolulu Harbor rather than attempting to remain at the entrance of Pearl. Fortunately, there were no casualties or incidents as the *Antares* sought refuge until the attack was over.

Ironically, just a few days before the bombing of Pearl Harbor, Charles had composed a handwritten letter to the Chief of the Bureau of Navigation requesting a copy of his discharge papers with a clarification of type of discharge—he required that for employment. This handwritten letter was dated December 3, 1941, and was delivered on December 5, 1941.

And just as ironic, Charles Jackson French's letter no doubt passed through the same office where Lt. Commander Harry Bauer worked—a foreshadowing of their paths crossing in even more significant ways in the coming days. And though there was mayhem at the Bureau due to the immediate onset of declared war, Charles received a typed confirmation letter on December 11 from the office of the Chief of the Bureau, who at the time was Admiral Chester W. Nimitz.

Nimitz did not remain head of the Bureau, however, for many more days. President Roosevelt had need of the calm and stoic Nimitz elsewhere. On December 17, the president hand-picked him personally to be Commander-in-Chief of the US Pacific Fleet.

And two days later, on December 19, Charles Jackson French was officially reenlisted in the United States Navy as a mess attendant 2nd class. What he had told Viola was correct and admittedly, it gave the now twenty-two-year-old a sense of pride to be back in the Navy. He had no quarrel with the Navy per se, even though he did feel unfairly treated in a couple of the incidents that had occurred, resulting in a few days of bread and water.

But the country was at war now. In a few weeks he learned the ship on which he would be stationed. After a mistake in orders, he was assigned initially to the USS *Little*; however, he wound up on her sister ship, the USS *Gregory*. French wondered who his commander would be; since he was now a mess attendant 2nd class, he realized he might have a bit of direct contact with him. One more thing French realized: having served on heavy cruisers previously, Charles recognized immediately that these smaller converted destroyers were virtually without significant offensive capabilities.

"Hey, you better hope we ain't getting into too much real war stuff!" he halfway joked to some of the younger mess attendants that showed up on the *Gregory*. However, rumors were already flying that these destroyer/transports would be doing special duty, if not in the very thick of things.

And in the months ahead, there would be sailors on this little ship who would one day say with wholehearted fervor, "Thank God French was with us!"

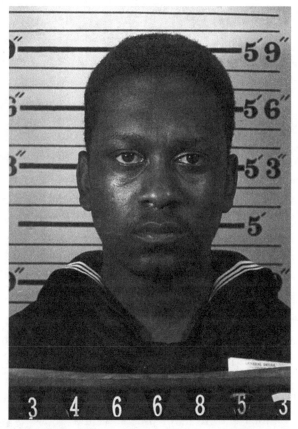

Enlistment photo of Charles Jackson French for his second period in the Navy, December 17, 1941, 5'8", 180 lb. Photo courtesy of Navy Military Archives (Golden Arrow Research).

CHAPTER 8

Green Dragons:
The Little Ships that Could

"Many are the plans in the mind of a man, but it is the purpose of the Lord that will stand." Proverbs 19:21

Christmas was different that December. Families still gathered around dinner tables, but conversation consisted of little else other than war. Young men were dressed in new uniforms, with satchels and duffel bags filling front hallways. Everything was at the ready to leave . . . after one last meal with parents, spouses, girlfriends, children. America stood firm as a nation forged together by a common resolve.

The Bureau of Navigation in Washington, DC busy on normal days, was now in hyperdrive: phones ringing continuously, every typewriter clicking with urgency, military members coming and going around the clock. Harry, always punctual, was now arriving even earlier and leaving later every day. New assignments came down daily, especially for those officers who were Academy-trained and who also held sea duty experience. Harry, along with so many others, waited anxiously wondering what his assignment might be. He didn't have long to wait.

On New Year's Day, January 1, 1942, Harry F. Bauer, the boy who had been so delighted to walk beside his distinguished Army father around Manila Bay and who had recently been promoted to Lieutenant Commander, received orders: "Proceed immediately to Naval Base San Diego and report to your immediate superior in command, if present, otherwise by message, for duty as . . ." He dashed off a call to Jackie with the words every aspiring seaman dreams of being able to say: "Honey,

I've been given a ship . . . the *Gregory*—she's a converted destroyer—carrying mainly troops and equipment right into the thick of things!"

Jackie could hear the excitement in his voice. "I'm happy for you, sweetheart," she said, a feeling of elation mixed with reality setting in. She was proud of her Navy husband, but it meant he would be leaving for war soon.

"Don't forget to come home early if you can," she reminded him.

"I won't. It's a very special day—tell my baby girl, Mimi, I'm headed home now and not to open her birthday presents until I get there!" With that, Harry pulled on his cover (Navy hat) and quickly left the building—a New Year's Day party with family and friends awaited. He had just been given command of a ship, and it was his daughter's seventh birthday—what a great day for a celebration.

Harry Bauer knew about the USS *Gregory*. Named after Admiral Francis Gregory, USN (1780–1866), she was laid down at Fore River Shipyard located on the Weymouth Fore River in Braintree and Quincy, Massachusetts, in August 1917. She had seen action in the Atlantic and Mediterranean during WWI before being decommissioned in July 1922 and entered the Philadelphia Navy Yard.

There, for two decades, the *Gregory* had waned, tied up in backwater areas, mothballed and fighting only rust. But her days of productivity were not yet over. She and a few dozen other similar destroyers were destined to play an indispensable role in WWII: among other duties, they would transport the legendary WWII Marine Raiders to their destinations, the bloody beaches of the Pacific where, eventually, the war was won.

Revitalization of these destroyers revealed forward-thinking strategy a few years before the bombing of Pearl Harbor. As time passed during the 1930s, conflict possibilities had heightened on a global scale—certain war loomed on the horizon. Some "heads-up" military leaders initiated what steps they could to meet that eventuality. Fortunately, several recognized one area of fundamental necessity: the impending need for **troop** transportation over water and consequently, amphibious landings.

The USS *Gregory* in its original configuration of four smokestacks before two were removed along with two boilers below deck. This was done to create space to transport Marine Raiders to their amphibious landings in the Solomon Islands. Photo courtesy of Navy Military Archives.

The Navy resorted to a group of WWI destroyers, mothballed for twenty years. The concept was to convert these smaller ships, called "flush-deckers," into transports. The nickname reflected their maritime design: a main deck that ran the length of the ship from stem to stern with no deck level change. Though this deck might have masts, guns, and other structures projecting upward from the deck itself, there were no raised or lowered deck surfaces either forward or rearward. Three classes of flush-deckers—the *Caldwell*, *Wickes*, and *Clemson*—had been mass-produced between 1917 and 1921 and formed the bulk of the destroyer navy.[*]

---

[*]   For more information see *The Famed Green Dragons: The Four Stack APDs*, Turner Publishing Co., 1998, 8.

Originally, these WWI destroyers had four smokestacks; therefore, they had four boilers with armament consisting of four 4-inch guns and twelve 21-inch torpedo tubes. To make room for troops, supplies, and landing boats, thirty-two of these flush-deckers were stripped of virtually all their armament, severely limiting their defensive capabilities. What little armament they did have varied slightly from ship to ship.

The armament that remained on the *Gregory* APD-3 consisted of three single three-inch/50 dual purpose gun mounts, two single 40mm AA (anti-aircraft) gun mounts, and five single 20mm AA gun mounts; in addition, there was one depth charge rack and four depth charge projectors.

Besides armament being significantly reduced, all the four-stack destroyers had two smokestacks removed plus boilers to accommodate

The USS *Gregory*, 1942, after conversion to a destroyer/transport with significantly reduced armament and painted in camouflage pattern. Photo: Naval History and Heritage command (history.navy.mil).

landing craft on one deck and troops below deck. In reality, however, this only created a limited amount of space to squeeze in all sorts of items such as bunks, wash basins, showers, toilets, personal equipment, and baggage.

These mothballed WWI flush-deckers were redesignated as APDs: "AP" for transportation (specifically, Auxiliary Personnel) and "D" for destroyer. In this specialized group of converted destroyers, the USS *Manley* was the first to undergo transformation beginning in late 1938 and officially redesignated by the Navy as an APD on August 2, 1940. Since the *Manley* was the first WWI destroyer to undergo conversion, she was numbered APD 1; the next converted destroyer was APD 2, then APD 3, and so forth. *

Another moniker for the destroyer conversions was "high-speed transports," an ironic label, since after removal of two stacks and boilers, their original speed was reduced from 34.75 knots to around 28 knots— or less. One captain answered the question of "What does APD stand for?" and with a wry grin replied, "It means 'All-Purpose Destroyer.'" And in Officers' Club bars, more than one young, aspiring naval officer was overheard joking about what they should be called. Occasionally, "ASD" was suggested: "All Sitting Ducks."

But despite their reduced defensive capabilities and speed, these converted destroyers would serve a vital role in the war, especially during the critical and vicious beginning of the Guadalcanal campaign. After the war, Nimitz would pay sincere, if not understated per his immutable manner, tribute to these lionhearted vessels: "With little means, these ships performed duties vital to the success of the campaign."

Four of the first few APDs formed part of a key unit of which Harry's ship, the USS *Gregory*, was a member. Transport Division 12 included,

---

* Alexander, Joseph H., *Edson's Raiders: The 1st Marine Raider Battalion in World War II*, Annapolis, MD: Naval Institute Press, 2001, 13; General Twining's quote from *No Bended Knee: The Battle for Guadalcanal*, Novato, CA: Presidio Press, 1996, 93.

among others, the USS *Colhoun* APD-2, the USS *Gregory* APD-3, the USS *Little* APD-4, and the USS *McKean* APD-5. These four ships, along with a handful of others, were destined for special duty, in particular the *Gregory* and the *Little*. The two sister ships would transport Carlson's Raiders to Midway, then assist in many other important Raider missions including delivering Edson's Raiders for the initial invasion in the Solomon Islands on August 7, 1942.

With their complement of eight to ten officers and one hundred or so enlisted, these "brave little ships," as they came to be called, were transport work horses and personified in steel the hearts of their brave crews and passengers. As many as 150 Raiders at a time—sometimes more—would be packed into each ship: personal belongings, weaponry plus equipment were all crammed into any nook and cranny that could be found.

Cramped quarters aside, the Raiders, especially Merritt Edson's 1st Marine Raider Battalion, developed a unique, close bond with the APD crews. Award-winning author and retired Marine Joseph Alexander writes about this special relationship in his detailed book documenting Edson's Raiders:

> If ever there were a marriage made in heaven it was the union between the 1st Marine Raider Battalion . . . and the first six converted high-speed transports, known as APDs ("Able-Peter-Dogs") in the phonetic alphabet of the time. Rarely has a single Marine outfit been so closely identified with the same squadron of ships for such an extended period. For more than two years the same APDs provided a seagoing home for Edson's Raiders. The small ships first provided experimental amphibious raid training along the Atlantic coast and in the Caribbean, then launched the Raiders in their initial combat action on Tulagi, transferred them to Guadalcanal, delivered them to their night landing at Rice Achorage, New Georgia, and then returned two months later to extract the emaciated survivors back to "civilization."

The Marines came to love the APDs—ship, captain, and crew. General Merrill Twining described them as "those heroic little ships."[*]

Although the APD program provided a solution to the Navy Department's need for small transports, the transformation process provided little of the most fundamental necessities for troop living, comfort, or sanitation. After removing two boilers on each flush-decker, a small cargo hold was created, not much more. "The first APDs contained no bunks, heads, showers, vent fans, galleys, or fresh-water evaporators to support 130 troops embarked for weeks at a time. These were intolerable conditions even for tough-as-nails Raiders."[†]

Vociferous complaints from the troops reached General Holland "Howlin' Mad" Smith, who then sent Colonel Graves B. Erskine to investigate. Erskine found the rumors to be completely true. In fact, the living conditions were horrendous. His report to General Smith eventually addressed some of these issues, and soon a few bunks appeared as did some wash basins, a tiny troop galley, and a few other amenities. However, conditions remained bleak: bunks were hung so close together that most occupants couldn't turn over and time in the shower amounted to approximately 37.5 seconds.

Marlin "Whitey" Groft, one of Edson's Raiders, recalled how these little ships would roll heavily even in moderate seas. This inevitably would turn over any receptacle that had been used by some poor soul who couldn't wait for his turn in the head—the line was always agonizingly long—or for puking from seasickness. Accompanied by the smells

---

[*] Ibid, 16.

[†] "On 1 February 1939, Manley carried out her first landing exercise. With final modifications, the Marines requested more fast transports and five flush-deck destroyers were pulled out of 'moth balls' and converted. On 2 August 1940, the officially designated APDs, *Manley* APD1, *Colhoun* APD2, *Gregory* APD3, *Little* APD4, *McKean* APD5 and *Stringham* APD6 were formed into Transport Division Twelve—TRANSDIV 12—and the rest is history." *The Famed Green Dragons: The Four Stack APDs, APD Destroyer Sailors of WWII*, 10.

of over 220 men, who often went without showering, these odors turned the hot, humid, tight spaces below deck into a stinking cauldron.

Often at night, because conditions below were so unpleasant, many Raiders would opt to sleep on deck, which made walking around topside in the dark especially tricky. To add to the experience, frequent waves sprayed and washed over everything. Still, "Whitey" Groft was able to say without hesitation that "we Raiders grew to love these little ships and their crews, and the swabbies retuned the sentiment."[*] The APD crews made up for these shortcomings with their congenial spirits and "can-do" attitude.

The close relationship between Raiders and APD crews began here, especially on the *Gregory,* the *Little,* the *Colhoun,* and the *McKean.* Though the Raiders would be going ashore to face combat, there was no denying that these ships would be in the throes of battle and almost defenseless besides. The crews, for their part, grew to respect these tough—and raucous—Raiders, wildly cheering them on as they left the APDs headed for bloody beaches.

The timeless bond of the sea developed between sailors and Raiders. Solid proof came in later years after the war. Surviving Marine Raiders would show up at APD reunions and become overwhelmed with emotion at the thought of the faithful little ships and their crews who sacrificed so much.

During the war, Raider special forces also came up with their own name for these converted destroyer-transports. Since the vessels had been painted dark green with brown and tan camouflage highlights, Raiders dubbed them Green Dragons. The name stuck.

Two of these sister ships had another important connection: Lieutenant Commander Harry Bauer, captain of the *Gregory,* had a long-standing, close personal relationship with the man who would now

---

[*] Groft, Marlin "Whitey" and Alexander, Larry, *Bloody Ridge and Beyond: A World War II Marine's Memoir of Edson's Raiders in the Pacific,* New York: Berkley, 2014, 31.

be commanding the *Little*—it was none other than his friend, classmate, and fellow faculty member, Lieutenant Commander Gus B. Lofberg Jr., known as "Swede."

USS *Little* APD-4, sister ship of the *Gregory*, after conversion to a high-speed transport. Her camouflage paint clearly seen along her side prompted Raiders to nickname these ships "Green Dragons." Photo courtesy of Navy Military Archives.

Like Harry, Lofberg was reared in a military family. He was the son of Commander Gustave Brynolf Lofberg, Sr., who was in charge of the Local Coast Guard Station in Racine, Wisconsin, from 1903 to 1914. But seafaring links didn't end with his father: Lofberg was also a lineal descendant of Leif Erikson.

Gus and Harry had graduated from the Academy the same year, Class of '27. Afterwards, both went to sea for a few years. Then, they each returned as part of the Academy faculty during the mid-thirties. Their lives had intersected at many points but none so joyously as when both families, the Bauers and the Lofbergs, welcomed baby daughters into the world during the same year, 1935, while still on staff at "The Yard."

In the late 1930s, however, their paths separated. Harry went to the Bureau of Navigation, admittedly a position at the hub of all things Navy. Gus Lofberg, on the other hand, was performing his own vital role for the war effort. At the Bausch and Lomb Optical Company, Rochester, New York, the brilliant young naval officer was heavily involved in critical development of top-secret, state-of-the-art lenses for field glasses, periscopes, a variety of specialized apertures as well as other wartime equipment.

Harry and Gus touched base by phone.

"Well, Swede," said Harry during their first phone call after learning the news that they each would command one of the important destroyer-transports. "Looks like we'll be in the same arena again! Headed for the Pacific would be my guess—sure hope you've got all our binoculars worked out! You wouldn't like to venture a guess as to where we're going, would you?"

Gus chuckled. He and Harry held many fond memories together since early midshipmen days at "The Yard": Gus, the consummate academic; Harry, the consummate, charismatic leader. After the bombing of Pearl Harbor, Gus had requested sea duty.

"Well," replied Gus, "don't know where we are going exactly, but you can be sure it's somewhere deep in the Pacific—somewhere that might have a field flat enough for B-17s! It's time we take a crack at those tramps!"

CHAPTER 9

Change of Command

"Blessed be the LORD, my rock, who trains my hands for war, and my fingers for battle . . ." Psalm 144:1

As Harry entered the Wardroom, every officer immediately stopped talking and stood to attention. He walked to the end of the table and looked around. "You may be seated," he said.

"It's an honor to be your new commander," began Harry Bauer. He paused for a moment, looking over the room at the seven officers who would be serving under him. Most appeared younger than he was, but two or three were his senior.

"Our nation has been attacked," said Harry. "We've been attacked by an enemy with more ships—*newer* ships," he hesitated with a slight raise of his eyebrows, "and more equipment than we have, at present anyway. But we will respond. We will meet our enemy head on and deliver whatever the Navy needs, wherever that need may be."

Again, Harry paused and looked directly at his men in his calm, self-assured manner. "And . . . we will be victorious." The conviction in his voice was unrelenting. His officers nodded and let out a few impromptu whoops and "Yes Sirs!" Their new commander continued. "I'm proud to be a part of this crew and this ship. The USS *Gregory* will do her part in bringing this victory to fruition." He then had each officer introduce themselves around the table before dismissing them from the Wardroom to return to duty stations.

Traditionally, varying degrees of ceremony accompany the Change of Command of a ship in the Navy. The extent of formality depends on personnel and circumstances. With the advent of a declaration of war and *post haste* being the order of the day, the outgoing commander of the USS *Gregory* had dispensed with the usual formalities: a band, dress uniforms, color guard, all hands on deck.

Instead, Commander William Drane Brown, who had outfitted the *Gregory* during the past year, had earlier given a brief statement of farewell and "congratulations on a job well done" to a group of her sailors and officers standing at attention on deck. Then he did what is always carried out during a Change of Command in the Navy regardless of circumstances: he read aloud his "formal orders relieving him of command" of the ship and ordering him to proceed to his next assignment. Brown's new duty assignment consisted of outfitting and commanding another destroyer, the USS *Nicholas*, a ship that would also prove instrumental in the Guadalcanal campaign.

When Brown finished reading his orders to the assembled company, Harry Bauer immediately stepped forward to read aloud *his* orders stating that he was now assigned as commander of the USS *Gregory*. At the precise moment Bauer finished reading orders, total authority for the entire ship had passed from one man to another on January 26, 1942.

The two men, William Brown and Harry Bauer, had known each other casually at the Academy—Brown was in Class of '23, a senior when Harry was an entering freshman. Commander Brown would eventually serve as Chief of Staff and Aide to ComCruDiv12 (Commander Cruiser Division 12) under Admiral Nimitz, Admiral Halsey, and General Douglas McArthur, and retire as a Rear Admiral.

Harry's relaxed demeanor drew warm welcomes from all the other officers. He gave hearty handshakes to those standing closest to him. "We'll meet in the Wardroom in fifteen minutes," he said to them, most of whom had already been part of the ship's complement for several weeks along with the majority of the crew.

"This way, Sir," said one of his lieutenants who escorted the new commander to his cabin: a tiny room with a small desk, chair, recessed bunk, a scaled-down leather couch, and small corner bath. His personal belongings had already been delivered, so Harry spent a few quick minutes unpacking clothes, toiletries, and the only indication of any life circumstances other than the Navy: a small framed photograph of Jackie sitting with Mimi on her lap.

Harry held the picture for a moment, thinking back to Mimi's birthday party. It had been only twenty-six days before but seemed much longer. Mimi was so proud and excited to be turning seven years old.

"Look, Papa," she had said, "I'm a really big girl now—and I can blow out my candles all by myself. I don't need your help anymore."

With that enthusiastic declaration of independence, she had taken a deep breath and blown them out with one gasp, instantly clapping her hands with little jumps of joy. Harry had thrown his head back laughing and swooped her up into his arms.

Taking one final glance at the picture, Harry whispered to himself, "You'll always be my baby girl no matter how old you are." Setting the photograph on the metal desk, he headed to greet his officers waiting in the Wardroom.

Sometimes referred to as Wardroom Country, this area is a markedly special piece of real estate on any ship in the United States Navy. Set aside for use by officers only, it represents, in many ways, all that Navy orthodoxy represents. These traditions are articulated in official Navy personnel documents. "The Wardroom: Naval Customs, Tradition, and Usage" states:

> A Wardroom should be comparable to a gentleman's club in its tone of behavior and conversation . . . The criterion of a wardroom is that it shall be one in which officers are proud to bring a distinguished guest at any time, and know that the guest will receive the same dignified hospitality that would be expected in a gentlemen's club or at a gentlemen's dinner.

This type of a Wardroom is not obtained except by the sincere cooperation of all members.*

The Customs and Etiquette, Chapter III of "The Wardroom," further illuminates what this unique area represents:

Wardroom country is each officer's seagoing home, a home in which he should be proud to entertain his relatives and friends. It is also his club where he may gather with his fellow officers for moments of relaxation, such as a discussion of the daily problems; a movie; radio program; or just a game of ace deuces over a cup of coffee. Whatever the event, it is a place where members should conduct themselves within the ordinary rules of propriety, common sense and good manners, in addition to observing the rules of etiquette founded on customs and tradition.†

The size of Wardroom Country varies depending on the ship's size. On the *Gregory*, a ship approximately 314 feet long and 31 feet beam or width amidship, this area was smaller than most. The room, approximately 20 by 14 feet, contained a narrow rectangular table positioned in the middle surrounded by small dining chairs. Three seated meals a day would be served here to the officers, the table draped with white linen and set with china and silver. If the commander needed to eat when not able to come to the Wardroom, a meal on a silver tray with china and linen napkins could be delivered to him by a steward whether on the bridge or in his cabin.

Along two walls, small leather sofas and a couple of lounging chairs offered additional seating. A linen-draped table at one end held a silver

---

* "The Wardroom, Navy Customs, Traditions and Usage," Section I-1 *NavPers* 10002-A, history.navy.mil.com.
† "The Wardroom, Customs and Etiquette," Section III.

urn with hot coffee available round the clock, and on either side were heavy white porcelain cups and saucers, a basket of fruit, and the makings for a simple peanut butter and jelly sandwich. A quick snack grabbed on the run helped keep many an officer awake during midnight watches topside.

The Wardroom was also where ship captains held meetings. On this day, after the reading of orders on deck, the officers had gathered in the Wardroom to hear the first greeting and comments from their new commander. When Harry entered the Wardroom, everyone stood to attention. He walked with self-confidence but had an open face that immediately put everyone at ease. As time progressed, these officers would come to greatly appreciate his commitment to them and his leadership style.

During the next few days after taking command of the *Gregory*, Harry Bauer spent the time familiarizing himself with his ship and crew. The converted destroyer-transport needed only a few more seamen to constitute a full complement. The Navy had tapped all possible resources to fill positions quickly on every ship available for service: The United States Coast Guard was drained almost immediately. Motor Mechanic Oswald Spencer Austin (later promoted to Chief) fell into that category, and he was one of the first enlisted men Bauer met.

Oswald had followed in the footsteps of his father, Pell Burrus Austin, a chief boatswain's mate in the Coast Guard. The senior Austin oversaw stations along a sizable stretch of coast from Virginia Beach to Oregon Inlet located between Cape Hatteras and Nags Head, NC. However, family ties to the ocean reached even further back. Oswald was actually born in the Keepers' Quarters of the Currituck Beach Lighthouse on November 7, 1916, where his grandparents lived. His grandfather was a member of the US Lighthouse Service for many decades, a branch of service that was eventually folded into the United States Coast Guard.

Growing up on the Outer Banks of the Carolinas, Oswald experienced everything a salt life environment offers. From the time he was born, boating, swimming, fishing, sand, and surf filled his days. When he finished eighth grade—the highest level provided by the local school—Oswald would have had to go to the mainland to complete high school. Instead, he chose to remain on the Outer Banks; for income, he began flushing out wild cattle living among the stands of yaupon, red cedar, cypress, sabal palmetto, and thick underbrush. Eventually, he had rounded up enough cattle to form a good-sized herd and made decent money selling them locally. Though the state of North Carolina wouldn't pass a law forbidding cattle to roam free on the Outer Banks until 1958, pressure was already mounting to ban the practice. Oswald decided it was time to get out of the cattle business and continue a family tradition: he joined the Coast Guard.

The twenty-five-year-old was an ideal fit for the recently reconfigured Green Dragons. He had sharp mechanical skills to help with the Higgins boats, which would play a key role in transporting troops from ship to shore. In addition, Oswald was knowledgeable in maneuvering craft from water to land. When Bauer arrived as the new commander of the *Gregory*, Oswald had already been onboard ship for several weeks.

When the two of them first met, Bauer immediately liked the young man, who was twelve years his junior. Bauer knew he was Coast Guard and appreciated the skills Oswald brought to the crew.

"We'll need all your expertise to get these Raiders to shore successfully, Austin," Lieutenant Commander Bauer said to him as soon as they first met. "You'll keep our landing craft running smoothly, I'm sure."

The landing crafts Bauer was referring to were mainly the Higgins boats loaded two on each side of the *Gregory*. These were lowered into the water from davits, mechanized cranes used for raising and lowering equipment when needed. The usual wear and tear of engines, gears, and all working metal parts plus the corrosive effects of saltwater kept mechanics busy. Oswald's mechanical skills would prove to be exceptional and highly crucial in the months ahead.

"I'll do my best, Sir," returned Oswald.

CHAPTER 10

Commander and Mess Attendant

"Know well the condition of your flocks, and give attention to your herds . . ." Proverbs 27:23

A few weeks after Charles Jackson French reenlisted, he received orders on March 23, 1942, to report to his assigned ship—the ship that would carry him into war. His papers initially listed the USS *Little* but almost immediately changed. He wound up on her sister ship, the USS *Gregory*. As Charles lugged his seabag aboard to report for duty, he wondered who the new commander of this ship would be.

One thing Charles didn't have to guess about. Once onboard the *Gregory*, he knew for a fact these smaller WWI converted destroyers were virtually without offensive capabilities. During his first enlistment, he had served on heavy cruisers twice as large as the *Gregory*. The young sailor recognized the defense status immediately—or lack thereof. After he had tossed his seabag on one of the narrow hanging bunks claiming it as his, he headed for the galley.

"Hey, ya'll better hope we don't meet up with any enemy cruisers!" he halfway joked with some of the younger mess attendants that showed up in the galley. "We ain't got enough ack-ack on this ol' tin can," he said, grinning, referring to the ship's firepower. All of them had heard the rumors circulating that these destroyer/transports would be doing special duty, most likely with special forces.

He had already begun familiarizing himself with the various compartments, closets, and drawers in the galley area when the Chief Steward approached him.

"Hey, you the new guy?" the Chief asked.

"Yessir," said Charles.

"You sound southern," remarked the senior steward.

"From Arkansas," answered French.

"Thought so," said the Chief. "I'm from New York. This's your second enlistment, right?"

"Yessir," returned the newest mess attendant on the ship.

"Well, French," the Chief continued, "I've got to check on a container of foodstuff—we're loading up today. I need you to go to the bridge and see if Commander Bauer wants some lunch. He usually likes a sandwich delivered to him, so's he can keep on working. Look sharp."

"Yessir," said Charles, who couldn't believe he would be meeting the commander first thing. He went over to a small locker in the corner, opened it, and pulled out a fresh white bib apron, then turned to locate the bridge.

"It can't be too hard to find on this ol' tin can," he chuckled to himself and headed amidship.

When Charles entered the bridge, he spotted the commander holding a pair of binoculars at one of the small round windows located along the curving outer wall of the bridge. Bauer immediately turned when he heard someone behind him, and French, standing at attention, requested permission to enter. "Mess Attendant French," the young sailor said.

"Stand at ease—you said 'French,' right?" said Bauer.

"Yessir. Charles Jackson French—only nobody calls me anything 'cept French. The Chief said you might want a sandwich, Sir," he said.

"Yes, I would. Bring me a grilled cheese," said Bauer, "and whatever piece of fruit you can round up."

"Yessir," said French, "I'll get that right up."

"You're new onboard, aren't you? Where are you from?" Bauer was always interested in getting to know those around him—a trait left over from as early as high school days when he was a cheerleader and editor of his high school yearbook.

"New to the *Gregory* but not new to the Navy, Sir. I reenlisted after them Japs bombed us on Pearl—I'd only been out a couple of weeks," French told his commander. "I's born and raised in Arkansas—well, mostly raised there. My folks were both gone by the time I was eleven. Moved in with my sis in Omaha and joined the Navy soon as I could," French rambled on. Bauer didn't mind. It was the sort of information the commander liked to know about those who worked for him.

"Sorry to hear that about your folks," said Bauer. "Hopefully, we can establish some unity on our ship. After all, we're going to war together." Bauer enjoyed talking to the spunky young man who was open and seemingly not afraid to share information—or his thoughts.

"Yessir," said French. "I'll get your lunch right away." He turned and headed back to the galley.

Bauer stood for a moment thinking about all the different stories of the men on the *Gregory*, young men like motor mechanic Oswald Austin, who had come over from the Coast Guard, and some like French, who had reenlisted for a second tour of duty. However, most of the crew was composed of young men brand new to the sea with a wide range of backgrounds, personalities, and skills. He felt a deep responsibility for all of them. And he was particularly grateful that sprinkled among them were several with previous experience, like Austin and French. With what he expected they would be facing in the Pacific, Bauer knew they were going to need it.

CHAPTER 11

Pacific Bound

". . . for the LORD your God is He who goes with you to fight for you against your enemies, to give you victory."
Deuteronomy 20:4

It was one of those late spring days in southern California, balmy yet crisp, with no hint of humidity, a perfect day to be on the water. The USS *Gregory*, docked in San Diego Bay, had nearly completed loading with supplies and equipment—everything necessary to put out to sea.

Throughout the previous summer and fall months of 1941, Marine Raiders had trained along the east coast, conducting exercises in conjunction with the Green Dragons. Following the attack on Pearl Harbor, many of these APDs were dispatched to San Diego where they were loaded with equipment and landing craft, notably rampless Higgins boats. At the same time, the first two battalions of the legendary Marine Raiders were formed: Merritt Edson's 1st Raider Battalion on February 16, 1942, then three days later, Evans Carlson's 2nd Raider Battalion.

However, it was not until the APDs and the 1st and 2nd Marine Raiders arrived in San Diego that practicing amphibious landings and maneuvers reached a fevered pitch. The *Gregory*, along with her sister ship, *Little*, spent countless hours cruising up and down the California shoreline working with Raiders in beach assault exercises. When they could, most of the ships' crews would watch from the rails as brawny Raiders strove to perfect their strenuous landing maneuvers.

Bauer especially enjoyed observing from the bridge wing, a small landing just outside the bridge. He knew what these guys would be facing once they arrived at their final destinations. And he knew the better prepared his ship and crew were to do *their* jobs, the better chance the entire operation had of succeeding.

Interaction between the *Gregory*'s crew and the Raiders was particularly critical when landing craft struggled for positioning beside the ship while Raiders grappled their way into them. A potentially dangerous maneuver, it required extreme strength and coordination: slipping over the ship's sides and down the rope nets, "hands on vertical lines only, feet on horizontal lines only." It took a Raider just once to experience the heavy boot of a guy above him smashing his fingers flat to remember that hands belonged only on the vertical lines while climbing down the ship's side.

But once at the bottom of the nets, there existed an even greater possibility for catastrophe. The Higgins boats, or any landing craft, rocked up and down, swaying and banging against the ship's side. Transitioning from nets to landing craft required extreme agility to avoid being crushed between the two. High seas, often the case, heightened the danger.

Marlin "Whitey" Groft, a member of Edson's Raiders (1st Marine Raider Battalion), would always remember the dangers involved, even just during training exercises with the APDs and rubber boats. Though the APDs might be anchored, they often rose and fell at least eight feet with the waves. This required Raiders in full gear weighing upwards of one hundred pounds to hover above the gyrating craft and try to time their drop at just the right second. If they judged correctly, the transition was only a step into the boat. If their timing was off, they could plummet down into equipment or another Raider, or worse, into the sea. The last option could spell utter catastrophe. "How we did not lose anyone, I will never know," said Groft in later years.

Then, after disembarking, each amphibious landing carried its own unique challenges. Changes in water depth, underwater configurations like coral reefs or rocks, currents, churning surf—any number of variables held potential to breed disaster. And all this just to make it to shore . . . where death awaited in hiding.

Finally, it was time to depart the home shores of San Diego and sail for open water. Hawaii was now their destination.

The Marine Raiders, once in Pearl Harbor, chomped at the bit to get going. The sight of destruction from the bombing remained visible everywhere. Ships could be seen lying where they had been anchored on that calamitous morning. And now welders and workers scrambled all over them to repair damages from that horrific day of destruction. All the Raiders wanted to do was to push further into the Pacific toward the enemy.

When rumors of a major naval engagement surfaced in June, Raiders were on high alert; in fact, two companies in 2nd Raider Battalion had already deployed to an unknown destination. However, as details of the Battle of Midway materialized, Harry Bauer was also issued orders to leave Pearl Harbor with his ship crammed full of 2nd Battalion Raiders.

One of the companies aboard the *Gregory* was under Maj. Oscar Peatross's command. This well-respected Raider would later retire as a Major General and in years following the war, would pen his iconic book, *Bless 'em All: The Raider Marines of WWII*. In it, Peatross gives firsthand accounts of the elevated anticipation all the Raiders experienced to "get the show on the road"—or in this case, "on the sea." He explains how the situation, being "stuck" in Hawaii, had elicited their disappointment:

"The Battle of Midway, however, was fought without the need for us to land or counterland, and we suffered a big letdown. But relief was not long in coming, and as Companies 'C' and 'D' returned from Midway on June 21, we were preparing to depart. Carlson's command group and Companies 'A,' 'B,' 'E,' and 'F' embarked in APDs *Gregory*, *Little*, *Colhoun*, and *McKean* and on June 22 headed northwest from Pearl Harbor toward an unannounced destination. I couldn't believe that we could be sailing toward the enemy and not yet know where we were going, but we were."[*]

After sailing from Hawaii for a few hours, Harry called to the Wardroom all his officers along with the Marine Raider officers on board. Peatross listened intently as Commander Bauer announced he had opened his secret orders. "Our initial destination is Midway," Bauer said. Even though the Battle of Midway was over, for all practical purposes, command authorities continued to view the area as vulnerable and on extreme high alert. Moreover, the Japanese might be planning another attack elsewhere in the Pacific.

The *Gregory* sailed for Midway during the last days of June 1942. During this round trip, the unique relationship which had been developing between her crew and the Raiders from 2nd Battalion, Carlson's Raiders, continued to materialize. Harry Bauer got to know all of the Raider officers and many of the enlisted men in 1st and 2nd Raider Battalions. And like the rest of his crew, he enjoyed immensely watching the agile warriors execute their strenuous training routines and hand-to-hand combat jousts on deck while at sea, weather permitting.

Once the *Gregory* arrived at Midway, however, the battle was over. The Japanese had never been able to invade the island, and their convoy of remaining ships had turned to sail back to Japanese waters. The engagement, a decisive victory for the United States, was a turning point of the war in the Pacific.

Though not participating in the actual Battle of Midway, this round trip from Hawaii to Midway and back solidified the wonderful camaraderie that was developing between the *Gregory*'s crew and the Raiders. Harry was gaining valuable information about his ship, his crew, and passengers. He enjoyed being around the feisty Raiders, especially Oscar Peatross. In Peatross's memoirs, he writes extensively about the mutual respect that developed between the *Gregory*'s crew (really all crews of

---

[*]   Peatross, Oscar, *Bless 'em All*, Tampa, FL: Raider, 1995, 21.

the APDs) and the Raiders, and especially between himself and her commander, Harry Bauer. Records Peatross:

> Our ship, the USS *Gregory* was one with which we were well acquainted. We had been aboard her many times while conducting amphibious training out of San Diego, and with a minimum of delay we were able to come to grips with the many tasks required of embarked Marines. Our cooks and messmen went to the galley for duty; BAR-men went to the Higgins boats hanging in the davits to serve as additional antiaircraft protection, a few Marines became helmsmen . . . our company doctor and his corpsmen set up in sickbay. Since the ship had no doctor of its own, the presence of our doctor and his corpsmen was particularly welcome and gave all hands an enhanced feeling of security, which was comforting inasmuch as we were sailing toward the enemy . . . on the fantail, a checkerboard was always set up, and there seemed always to be someone playing. Being the on-board checkers champion, I frequently was called on to defend my title and took on challengers in what spare minutes I had for play. Acey-Deucey, pinochle, and other card games were also popular pastimes among the embarked Raiders.[*]

Besides working together for onboard duties, a friendly competition developed among sailors and Raiders. Bauer encouraged all the various activities and enjoyed, as he always had, good relations with both officer and enlisted, sailor and Marine. To further provide activity, Harry authorized the use of balloons for target practice. Peatross's account of how that happened paints the scene:

> Conditions permitting, weather balloons were released twice a day to provide targets for small-arms antiaircraft firing

---

[*] Ibid., 22.

practice. Competition was keen among the BAR-men, and there were loud cheers for those who got hits and equally loud boos for those who missed. Competition was keenest, however, between the crews of the two forward, port and starboard, fifty-caliber antiaircraft machine guns. One was manned by Raiders and the other by sailors, and here the lines were sharply drawn. Initially the sailors were the better marksmen, but this was short lived. The Raiders drilled and drilled with their mount until they became real sharpshooters and soon were manning both mounts.[*]

Though the Battle of Midway was over and things had settled down substantially by the time these Raiders arrived there, nonetheless, the round trip out of Pearl had been a favorable learning experience for both sailors and the Marine Raiders on this Green Dragon. In later life, Major General Peatross recalled his admiration for the ship and especially for her commander. He often said that Lieutenant Commander Harry F. Bauer was "a fine officer and a true gentleman whom Company 'B,' 2nd Raiders had come to know and admire during their round trip to Midway aboard the *Gregory*."

From training and sea duty, there evolved between the two groups—APD crews and Raiders—admiration and respect for what each was contributing towards the war effort—a congenial relationship occasionally lacking between sailors and Marines. Many friendships developed that would endure a lifetime. The experience provided a practical test of Mark Twain's declaration: "There ain't no surer way to find out whether you like people or hate them than to travel with them."

Travel together they did. Halfway around the world in quarters so cramped many had to share bunks, food, clothing, equipment. And before it was all over, many would also share the ultimate bond—the shedding of blood together.

---

[*] Ibid., 23.

CHAPTER 12

Remembering: Spring 1993

". . . I remember you upon my bed and meditate on you in the watches of the night for you have been my help . . ."
Psalm 63:6

"Doggone this printer!" muttered Bob Adrian, trying to wrestle jammed papers from the lower section of his copier. After several unsuccessful attempts, he contacted his son, Jim, to come over and "unjam this contraption!"

After Jim Adrian left work, he headed to his parents' home—the lovely house next to the Naval Academy where he had grown up. Jim opened the door to the basement. Immediately, the familiar pipe smell wafted in the air, growing stronger the closer he neared his dad's wardroom. As he picked his way carefully down the shadowy, narrow steps, then into the tight corridor, he felt he was entering sacred passageways of ships his dad had served on.

Once inside the small office, the usual stacks of papers and books were here and there, the heavy ashtray was full of used pipe tobacco, and an empty Navy coffee mug sat off to one side awaiting the next cuppa brew, always black. It didn't take Jim long to get everything back in working order, then he stretched out on the cot for a quick visit.

"This bed's still warm!" he observed.

"Ha! You should've been on the *Gregory*!" laughed Bob. The Adrian family knew the story well, in fact, had heard it many times; the retelling still never failed to draw chuckles all around.

After Bob Adrian had graduated from the Naval Academy in June 1942, he and Joan had just returned home to Ontario, Oregon, from their glorious weekend with friends in New York City after his graduation from the Naval Academy. His dad had greeted him at the front door with a telegram in his hand. "Report immediately to San Francisco for shipping out to catch up with the USS *Gregory*," which had already sailed—a sure indication of the urgency of her mission. Bob and his dad jumped into their family car and headed south. The great adventure was about to begin.

In later years, his family would learn a highly touted Navy term that Bob had experienced personally on his very first ship: the dubious art of "hot-bunking." A ship packed with many more sailors than available beds creates a necessity: sharing sleeping spaces. When one sailor arises from a bunk, the next sailor quickly jumps in. The wrinkled sheets are ready and warm.

"You should've been on the *Gregory*," Bob repeated, thinking back to that day when he saw the converted destroyer-transport, ADP-3, for the very first time. He would never forget that initial encounter on the high seas: the ship, the crew, and particularly the Skipper, Harry F. Bauer, who taught him so much about running a ship and being a leader of men—and who gladly received the young ensign aboard with a broad smile and the unceremonious greeting of "We really don't have room for you but welcome aboard anyway!"

CHAPTER 13

One More Shipmate

"Let your eyes look directly forward and your gaze before you . . ." Proverbs 4:25

Success at the Battle of Midway bolstered the spirits of the nation and its entire military apparatus. At the same time, it provided impetus for the defeated enemy to seek to strengthen its positions in the South Pacific. Not surprisingly, British and Australian coast-watchers soon reported these accelerated operations by the Japanese, especially in the Solomon Islands.

At the highest levels in Washington, strategic planners were vigorously considering when and where the United States would launch its first offensive against Japan. Admiral Nimitz had already alerted large numbers of ships, first to San Diego, then to Hawaii, next to the rapidly expanding base at Noumea in New Caledonia.

Major General Alexander A. Vandegrift, commanding general of the 1st Marine Division, was operating under premises which he had been led to believe: that he would have until late 1942, or perhaps early 1943, to get his Marines ready for combat. When he received a warning order on June 26 to prepare his division for combat operations in the southern Solomons by August 1, one can only imagine his response. After the war, Major General Oscar Peatross speculated in his memoirs, "Surprise was undoubtedly the mildest of his (Vandegrift's) emotions."[*]

---

[*] Peatross, Oscar, *Bless 'em All*, 5.

As more and more Marines were hastily readied for an invasion, more ships of all stripes were also outfitted and manned for the invasion convoy. Consequently, the Navy continued to plug officers into crews whenever and wherever possible. Third-year Naval Academy Midshipmen were accelerated to graduate status in June of '42 instead of completing their fourth year in 1943. To accomplish this, they completed as many critical courses as possible during spring semester, then were sent packing off to war.

Robert Nelson Adrian was one of these graduates. The neophyte Ensign Adrian arrived on the *Gregory*, which had sailed from Hawaii further westward, in a singularly unusual way: suspended from a high-line boatswain's chair swinging from one ship to another. He was received, not with applause but loud boos. In his own words, later Captain Bob Adrian recounts his own unusual—and unwelcome— entrance into the war:

"Joan and I arrived home on the train from New York, and my dad handed me a telegram from the Navy Department to report immediately to San Francisco for transportation to the War Zone. I kissed my Mom and Joan goodbye, grabbed my suitcase and Dad and I left immediately. Two days later (they must have been waiting for me!) I was on the troop ship USS *President Adams* with a large convoy leaving San Francisco to join our naval forces gathering at New Caledonia for the invasion of Guadalcanal: the first big step on the planned push to Tokyo.

"We stopped at Suva, Fiji Islands, to pick up more ships for the convoy. About a day after that I heard my name on the ship's public address system directing me to report to the transfer station where I would be transferred with my cruise box of gear, to the destroyer *Gregory* that was refueling alongside the *Adams*. My large cruise box was filled with the usual but also included all the memorabilia that accompanies a Naval Academy grad plus my dress whites and my sword and scabbard.

"The *Gregory* was one of 12 (6 Pacific Fleet and 6 Atlantic Fleet) older destroyers that were converted to High Speed Transports, each to carry a company of the Marine Raider Battalions (6 of them in our group) on raids behind enemy lines. They had removed 1 Fire Room and

Engine Room (leaving the DDs with one engine room and fire room to operate 1 instead of 2 screws—but they could still make 28 knots with that screw—a standard destroyer with 2 screws—a fire room and engine room for each screw—could make 35 knots). They made troop quarters for 1 company of Raiders in these former fire room/engine-room spaces and had mounted 4 fast Higgins boats (2 each side) housed in rapid operating davits which could quickly load and launch a company of Marine Raiders for raids behind enemy lines.

"When I was being passed over to the *Gregory* in a high-line boat-swain's chair, I got continuous loud boos from the *Gregory*'s Raiders and crew who were topside. I was just what they didn't want—a fresh caught Naval Academy ensign with a big box of his gear (they had no room or bunk to assign me!) as they were preparing for their invasion of Guadalcanal in only a few days. When I got aboard and we peeled away from the *Adams* on the completion of fueling, I was taken to the Bridge to meet the captain of the ship—LCDR Harry F. Bauer, USN out of the Class of '27 at the Academy. He confirmed that they really had no room for me in Officer's Quarters but would put my cruise box in a 20mm clip shack (a space under each of the 4 anti-aircraft 20mm Guns where they clipped the 20mm ammunition). He said to take what I needed to live with (khaki uniforms, skivvies, etc) and put them in a seabag and they could find somewhere in Officers' Country to store it and I could "hot bunk" when I was off duty (find an empty bunk to sleep in of someone who was on watch). He assigned me as a Junior Officer for one of the Bridge Watches. He also informed me that we (*Gregory*) were proceeding to join the invasion forces of the Japanese held Island of Guadalcanal (the largest island in the Solomon Island chain). D-Day was scheduled for August 7, which was in two weeks.

"The next day we arrived in New Caledonia to join the invasion forces already there, and I was amazed to see the number of ships which made up this force."*

---

* Robert Adrian's personal journals.

The young ensign was not the only one who found the sight of so many ships gathering in a dazzling South Pacific harbor exhilarating. Mess attendant French stood near the *Gregory*'s bow smoking a cigarette while the "smoking lamp was lit" before the nonstop bustle of dinner prep. French took a deep drag on his Camel, wishing it was a shot of whiskey instead. Few circumstances in life are more conducive for reflection and meditation than the days and hours leading up to an impending—and no doubt savage—battle.

As he looked over the exotic landscape of water rapidly filling up with a massive convoy, he thought back to his childhood in southwestern Arkansas. He had had several friends around his age, all of them in the same circumstances—poor and often hungry, mostly barefooted, with no toys or athletic equipment to use. Together, they manufactured play from rough-and-tumble antics, running through the woods, throwing rocks, gathering sticks, hide-and-go-seek, catching fireflies at dusk, then filling jars with holes punched into their metal tops. All the youngsters were spunky and agile. French could climb anything.

He thought about those days in the country and suddenly remembered a small wooden structure on the edge of town where he and his friends often raced to see who could be first to scramble up on its shingled roof. It had been a small Coca-Cola and ice stand at one time. Once they were on top, French and his friends pretended they were standing aboard a mammoth vessel sailing beyond the seas. Now, here he was on the deck of a large ship, granted not as large as some ships he had been on during his first enlistment, but larger than a Coca-Cola shack.

As he gazed over the warm tropical waters beneath the *Gregory*, French reminisced about the Red River, which had formed such a key component of his childhood landscape. And he thought about his day of epiphany—that first day he had discovered the secret of water. It would hold a body up if you didn't fight it, and a person could float with little movement—what's more, stay afloat. He laughed to himself thinking about some of the white sailors, especially one from Alabama, who said he didn't believe French could swim. "He don't know it, but I can," whispered French to himself with a sense of pride in his unrecognized ability, which had been loudly discredited by his Alabama shipmate.

About that time, Commander Bauer and Mechanic Austin, the crew member from the Coast Guard, appeared on deck. They walked over to one of the Higgins boats to inspect the davit. French could hear Austin explaining to Bauer why they had experienced trouble earlier in the day lowering one of the Higgins boats down to the water below.

"All I want to know is can you get this thing repaired tonight?" asked the commander. "We're headed to Koro tomorrow for a final rehearsal before the invasion. All the top brass will be there."

"Yes, Sir, I can," replied Austin. "But I'll need some light, Sir."

"Well, get some men to hold a tarp over you—let's not create any targets in case we get enemy aircraft overhead tonight . . . but let's get it done. We need it fully operational by tomorrow morning," said Bauer in his usual friendly, yet authoritative way.

"Aye, aye, Sir. Will do." Austin turned to locate a tarp and a couple of "holders."

As Bauer was about to leave the deck, he noticed French standing at the rails. "It's quite a sight out there, isn't it, French?" he called over to the young steward and nodded his head toward the ever-amassing convoy.

"Yessir, you sure can believe that," French said with his ever-present enthusiasm.

"We'll be headed to our destination very shortly," said the commander. "We're part of the greatest invasion in our history. That's something to think about."

"Yessir," said French. "Them Japs'll soon know who we are."

"Yes, they will. You can count on it, French," returned Bauer with total confidence.

Suddenly, the young mess attendant remembered what time it was and that he had been lingering at the rails far longer than he should. "Would the Skipper like me to fetch something to the bridge for supper?" he quickly asked.

"Yes—do that. Can you find me a bacon sandwich somewhere?" said Bauer.

"Yessir, sure can," said French. "Comin' right up."

French hurried off to get a bacon sandwich squared away for the commander. He would soon have it ready to serve on a heavy white porcelain plate edged with narrow dark blue stripes and a blue anchor painted at the plate's top; these he would place on a small silver tray lined with a crisp, white linen napkin to carry to the bridge.

The commander watched the young man hustling down the steps and lingered at the rails for a moment. He looked out over the waters and thought about his crew. The *Gregory* had trained hard with the Marine Raiders. Every man on his ship knew their job and did it well. The same was true for the Raiders. Harry had never seen such dedication to physical fitness, agility, and fighting strength as with these Marine special operational forces. He realized fully that they were preparing for possible hand-to-hand combat and that whatever happened, these Raiders wouldn't back down.

Just as the gravity of the moment had caused French to reminisce about family and friends back in Arkansas, the thirty-seven-year-old's thoughts quickly turned homeward also. It had now been about seven months since he had seen his wife, Jackie, and their sweet daughter, Mimi. It had been only a few days past Mimi's seventh birthday when he had left for San Diego and then war in the Pacific. Getting command of his own ship was something Harry had worked for and finally achieved. But it was bittersweet. He knew without a doubt that the APDs would be performing a key and vital role in the coming invasion, albeit a very dangerous one. His friend of many years, Gus Lofberg, was in command over on the *Little*. They both recognized and had discussed the limitations of their ships—the lack of any substantive fire power to defend themselves or carry out a serious offensive. And they each knew exactly where they had to sail in order to land these brave Marine Raiders—behind enemy lines on a little-known island far, far away.

Night was rapidly falling. He looked upward where a few stars were already glowing. "Watch over my little family while I'm gone, Father God," he whispered, "and give us victory."

CHAPTER 14

Dress Rehearsal

"He trains my hands for battle, so that my arms can bend a bow of bronze." 2 Samuel 22:35

Superstition purports that a disastrous dress rehearsal bodes well for a successful opening night. By those standards, the invasion of the Solomons was guaranteed victorious, since the final few days of simulated practice landings exemplified another well-known quip: "If it can go wrong, it will go wrong."

General Vandegrift was more definitive in his evaluation: "It was a complete bust—a fiasco." Executive Officer Sam Griffith, of 1st Marine Raider Battalion, described their performance as "shocking." Griffith meant shockingly awful. He further stated that it was "the only time in my life that I ever saw Edson despondent."*

The four APDs (Transport Division 12), *Colhoun, Gregory, Little, McKean,* that would be involved in delivering the 1st Raider Battalion on shores held by the enemy for the invasion of the Solomons had arrived in Noumea, New Caledonia. As the war progressed, Noumea would become the primary forward base for US military operations throughout the South Pacific during WWII.

On July 24 most of 1st Marine Raider Battalion, commanded by Col. "Red Mike" Edson, embarked except for a small rear echelon that

---

* Hoffman, Jon T., *Once a Legend: "Red Mike" Edson of the Marine Raiders,* Novato, CA: Presidio, 1994, 175.

joined later. The projected number of Raiders was 140; this was added to an APD crew of 100–120 members plus 8–10 officers. But the troop number exceeded what had been estimated by at least 10–15 men. Raider Oscar Peatross noted in his memoirs that "as always, the APD skippers and crews were very cooperative and helpful in making space in their already cramped quarters for the Raiders and the extra loading generated no interservice disharmony."[*]

On July 26, the fully crammed APDs headed back to Koro in the Fiji Islands to participate in a final rehearsal. Peatross provides an account of the scene:

> About 400 miles or so south of Fiji, all those Raiders who were on deck were treated to a sight they would long remember. On the horizon, the silhouettes of other ships began to appear, and as the afternoon wore on, more and more ships could be seen at all points of the compass. By nightfall, virtually every ship-type in the US Navy was represented: almost eighty ships including an air support force built around the aircraft carriers *Saratoga*, *Enterprise*, and *Wasp* and the battleship *North Carolina*; a covering and bombardment force of cruisers and destroyers, a minesweeper group, and a transport group of nineteen transports and four APDs carrying almost 20,000 Marines—only a few less than the total strength of the Marine Corps three years earlier.[†]

Quite possibly, it was the sight of all these ships that inspired some anonymous Raider bard to compose a commemorative verse for "Bless 'em All":

> They sent for the Navy to come to Tulagi;

---

[*] Peatross, Oscar, *Bless 'em All*, 33–34.

[†] Ibid., 5.

The Navy responded with speed.
In 10,000 sections, from sixteen directions,
Oh, Lord, what a screwed-up stampede.

Although the maneuvering of the ships into their positions in the convoy might have seemed "a screwed-up stampede," to the spectator, it was vitally crucial regarding the security of the strongest amphibious task force ever assembled by the United States up to that time. Soon, however, the ships were herded into place, and a course was set for the Fijis—the area of their final rehearsal.

The convoys arrived off Koro on July 28, 1942, and for the next four days, the Marines and Marine Raiders practiced clambering down the cargo nets into the landing craft, and the boat crews practiced assembling into formations and taking their positions for the ship-to-shore movement, but without landing. The rehearsal plans initially had called for landing on the beach of Koro; however, as the first few boats grounded on the coral reef surrounding the island, this part of the plan was quickly scrubbed. The need to conserve the few available landing craft, many of which were already in poor shape, precluded any further attempts at realistic practice landings.

As best they could under such artificialities, air and naval gunfire elements practiced coordinating their operations with the landing. Finally, to the ineffable relief of Marines bored with clambering up and down cargo nets and circling for hours in Higgins boats, the exercises concluded. Vandegrift wasn't at all impressed with how the rehearsal had gone but later reneged slightly and said "they weren't that bad."*

The time had come. After dusk on July 31, the entire force got underway for the objective area, the carrier task force to the south and west and the amphibious task force to the west toward the Coral Sea. The unpracticed, unrehearsed, and poorly equipped 1st Marine Division was en route for its date with destiny. The 1st Marine Raider Battalion,

---

* Ibid. 35.

however, under the hard-charging Edson, was fine-tuned, tough, and completely braced to confront whatever challenge came their way. It was the first US amphibious invasion since the Spanish-American War.

Standing in the *Gregory*'s bridge, Harry Bauer, son of an Army soldier who had fought in the Spanish-American War, pulled the 1MC (main circuit: internal shipboard communications system) from the intercom to deliver a message to his crew. As the crew listened intently to their commander's calm, encouraging voice, the massive convoy of ships began once more to form up.

"On the *Gregory*, this is your captain. We are underway with the largest invasion convoy in our history—to deliver our warrior brothers, the 1st Marine Raiders, to their destination in the Solomons—Tulagi Island to be exact, currently held by enemy special forces—but not for long! This is what we have all trained for, and I'm confident that each of you will do your job to the very best of your abilities. May God be with the *Gregory* and the Raiders, grant us safe passage . . . and victory."

CHAPTER 15

A Swindle

"A merchant, in whose hands are false balances, he loves to oppress." Hosea 12:7

"Appearances can be deceiving" is a well-known cliché, but truthful nonetheless, especially concerning the Solomon Islands. Best-selling author and military historian Richard F. Newcomb added a sinister edge when he said these remote islands had always been a swindle. Like a string of emeralds stretching across deep blue velvet, their shores promise one thing, but their dark interiors deliver quite another.

Present day Ironbottom Sound, the largest maritime gravesite in the world. Photo from the personal collection of Barbara Witte.

Discovered by Spanish explorers in 1568, the islands unfolded their mysteries, one grotesque event after another. Cannibals greeted one of the first eager landing parties with the half-eaten torso of a native boy—as a gift. On another exploration into the interiors, Spanish scouts were set upon by stones and spears thrown from the cover of thick vegetation; many were killed on the spot, survivors having to leave their countrymen where they fell, presumably to the fate of the native boy.

The swindle began in an unlikely place—Peru. Tupac Inca Yupanqui, a ruler of the Inca Empire in the late 1400s, supposedly sailed westward in thirty or more balsas with sails and discovered many of the South Pacific Islands. They brought back to South America gold and a bronze chair, among other treasures.

During the following century, celebrated Spanish navigator, Pedro Sarmiento de Gamboa, on one of his own voyages to Peru, heard these tales of the Islands of Solomon, so-called by the Incas, because whatever isles had been discovered reminded them of the biblical King Solomon's mines and wealth. When de Gamboa returned to Spain, he convinced King Philip II to sponsor an expedition that would sail the "600 leagues west of Peru" deep into the South Pacific. Alvaro de Mendana de Neira was appointed to lead it and Herman Gallego selected as chief pilot.

Ironically, some historians doubt whether Tupac Inca had ever sailed westward, and even if he did, had discovered any gold or other treasures. Some say the Spanish explorers were following, at best, a legend to begin with. At any rate, after weeks of crossing "waters without end"—the Pacific has seemed the same to most voyagers across its nearly 6,000 miles—de Neira and Gallego finally spied a small speck on the horizon. They began navigating through these islands, naming each one along the way; Gallego was sent ahead in a separate ship to explore further south.

After navigating a channel filled with tricky crosscurrents and dark waters, he came upon the largest island in the group. On board ship was a man named Pedro de Ortega Valencia, called the Master of the Camp, with some forty men whose purpose was to land and explore. Ortega called the newly discovered island Guadalcanal, after his lovely little village homeplace in southern Spain. The landing party found nothing of value except some roots and fruit, and a half-eaten human torso. On a subsequent trip to the island, they were attacked by natives and nine of their party were killed. Though these intrepid explorers had discovered what had been dubbed the Solomon Islands, they found nothing there to reflect the auspicious name. The Spanish never returned.

Historian Newcomb describes it this way:

> Everywhere in [these] islands it was the same. The natives were hostile and the land was hostile, refusing to yield gold, or silver, or gems, or even food. This land, that looked so rich, was not only poor but belligerently poor, teeming with decay and putrefaction. In the rain forests the rotting vegetable matter gave off revolting vapors and the jungles abounded with strange and deadly reptiles, huge rats, and a species of giant frog weighing three pounds. The waters, so blue and benign by day, turned black at night, and swift and treacherous currents ran among the islands. There was nothing in this whole place but frustration and foreboding, and the men (Spaniards) cheered when they learned they were going home.*

Some five hundred years later, men would cheer once more when informed they were leaving Guadalcanal, only to discover ever-increasing horrors on the next island . . . and the next. But ships and men wouldn't exit these dark waters off Guadalcanal without paying a terrible price for their release.

The distance between Fiji Islands and the Solomons is about 1,400 miles as the crow flies. On July 31, 1942, the lengthy convoy steamed first south away from Fiji, then turned northward. During the journey, officers pored over maps they had available, such as they were, and

---

* Newcomb, Richard F., *The Battle of Savo Island*, New York: Henry Holt, 1961, 8.

looked through their scant intelligence of an area none of them had ever visited before.

When General Vandegrift had received his warning order in June, he sent his intelligence officer, Lieutenant Colonel Frank Goettge, to Australia to gather as much information as possible about these remote islands. Goettge discovered that the Japanese had established an area headquarters on Guadalcanal, where they were nearly finished constructing an airfield. Troop strength plus workers was estimated at around 5,000, which turned out to be somewhat high.

Compared to this meager information, what was known of the small island named Tulagi, lying about twenty miles across the channel just off Florida Island, seemed voluminous. This was partially due to the fact that past residents were contacted about the island, which had been the center of the British Protectorate. The topography, landscape, government buildings, a prison structure, and even its nine-hole golf course were mostly well documented. It was also learned that here, Japan had stationed a few hundred of its special forces. These combatants were on average taller than the regular line Japanese soldier, most about six feet in height and better trained, especially in hand-to-hand combat.

Harry, as well as many others in the convoy, had already seen sea duty in the Pacific. And since his father had been stationed in the Philippines, traveling across the seas didn't seem daunting. The same was true for French, as this was his second enlistment, and he had crossed the equator before. Many of the young men, however, were new to the sea altogether. Likewise, many had never been to an island until their duties commenced on the *Gregory*.

For inexperienced seamen, or neophytes, these days headed to the unknown Solomons crawled along—and over all this loomed the fear and heavy specter of going to war. Harry had informed all his officers, along with senior chiefs, to remind the entire crew to tread softly during their watches and speak in whispers if they needed to speak at all. He slept little on the journey to the remote Solomons, and French was diligent in keeping him supplied with bottomless mugs of hot coffee.

As for the Marine Raiders, they were as antsy as any but for different reasons. They were impatient to be about their business, eager to do what they had been training for months to do: fight and defeat the enemy. They spent their time cleaning and recleaning their weapons, packing and repacking gear, writing letters home, some reading whatever books were available; for many it was their pocket Bibles.

But one thing Harry and all the other commanders throughout the convoy couldn't have been more pleased with was the extremely unfavorable weather conditions—which meant an excellent state of affairs for an invasion. Every day since they had sailed away from Fiji, the sky had been overcast with dark clouds, misting rain, sometimes pouring, and continual, heavy fog. The worst day was the day before the scheduled landing: a fine day for a surprise attack.

During the night of August 6, 1942, the convoy of ships loaded with the invasion forces of Marines and Marine Raiders, officially known as Operation Watchtower, steamed through rolling seas past the western side of Guadalcanal, heading northward. Once at the northern tip of Guadalcanal Island, the task force rounded that point called Cape Esperance and entered Savo Sound in silence and undetected.

The Sound was so named because of a very small, almost perfectly round island with jagged edges, lying in the middle of the northern portion of the channel. These waters feed into a larger body traditionally known as Sealark Channel, which flows between Guadalcanal and the smaller islands of Tulagi, Gavutu, Tanambogo, and Florida Island, lying to the east.

In the weeks and months to come after the initial invasion on August 7, 1942, catastrophic clashes one after another—mostly at night—peppered these waters. The wreckage of ships and vessels of all sizes, planes, equipment, materiel, war vehicles, trucks, cannons, half-tracks, weapons, and unexploded ordnance paved the floor of the channel. Beyond these symbols of war, which could be replaced, the bottom also became the silent, dark resting place of well over a thousand men.

To this day professional and amateur divers alike have explored less than half of the numerous wreckage sites. Extreme depths—400–600 fathoms in some places and swift currents in others—have often hindered these efforts. Though there has been some accurate identification of certain vessels, many have never been ID'd or even located, and probably never will. The men who perished in these bloody waters remain where they came to rest.

Even before the war was over, the channel was given a new name indicative of its new, unique nature—Ironbottom Sound. It remains the largest naval, air, and materiel gravesite in the world—and the site of the largest US naval disaster in history. The initial entrance into the area early on August 7, 1942, was a swindle, just like these islands had always been: a deceptively easy and uneventful entry. The dark waters of Hell's midnight lay silent . . . waiting.

CHAPTER 16

Bombardment and the Battle
Breakfast: August 7, 1942

*"I pursued my enemies and destroyed them, and did not turn
back until they were consumed." 2 Samuel 22:38*

After rounding the northern tip of Guadalcanal in the predawn hours
of August 7, eight months to the day after the bombing of Pearl
Harbor, the convoy maneuvered south. Guadalcanal lay to starboard
(right) and the small island named Tulagi to port (left).

Immediately, the convoy then split into two groups. One group,
called Task Force Group X-Ray, passed south of Savo Island to position
themselves facing their designated landing beach, code-named Red
Beach. This group transported the 18,000+ regular line Marines from
1st Marine Division.

The other group called, Task Group Yoke, passed outside Savo Island
and headed for Tulagi, the destination for the Marine Raiders under the
command of Merritt Edson. They would land in column at H hour
(0800) at their landing area, code-named Beach Blue; meanwhile, the
1st Marine Parachute Battalion would head out (by boat) at H plus 4
hours for the smaller islands of Gavutu, then seize Tanambogo. The
APDs carrying Edson's Raiders continued their slow and methodical
sailing towards Tulagi at about 10 knots.

Before they had entered the channel to approach their holding point,
Harry and his entire crew had donned helmets and life jackets. Now, in
the low red glow of the nighttime bridge light, he stood close to the
helmsman, speaking softly and only when absolutely necessary. He held

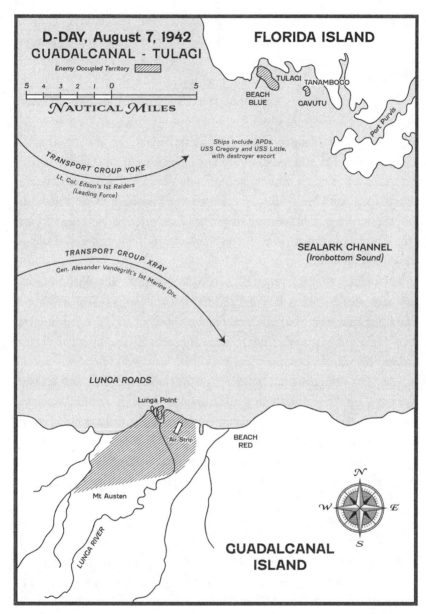

Overall view of Operation Watchtower showing approach by US troops to Guadalcanal and Tulagi, D-Day, August 7, 1942. Edson's 1st Marine Raiders were transported by APDs including the USS *Gregory* and USS *Little*.

his binoculars, at intervals stepping out onto the bridge wing, peering into the foggy darkness. Every nerve in his body was tensed, though outwardly he maintained his calm, stoic demeanor. They had made it this far, totally undetected by the Japanese.

In the galley, cooks and mess attendants had made a special effort to serve a delicious, hot breakfast as a send-off meal, which they rolled out by 4:30 a.m. Calling it their "Battle Breakfast," cooks served steak and eggs, biscuits and toast, a variety of jellies, jams, and fruit. As they left the galley, French said "Give 'em hell—seeya tonight—we're havin' chocolate cake!" He made a special point of wishing "Good luck" to Sid, the white guy from Alabama who didn't believe he could swim. "Y'all be careful, you hear, out in them waters!" French called out to some of the Raiders.

"Don'cha worry, Frenchie," Sid called back to him with his own southern accent. "They'll be back! They know how to swim." Sid never passes up an opportunity to chide French about his supposed swimming prowess. Looking over at the Raiders, he winked and laughed, "That colored boy thinks he can swim!"

At 6:30 a.m., the naval gunfire and air strikes erupted. The cruiser, *San Juan*, led the way with an initial five-inch shell followed by 280 more. 1st Marine Raider, Marlin "Whitey" Groft, likened it to a deadly Fourth of July celebration. Two destroyers from their Task Force, the *Monsoon* and the *Buchanan*, joined in also delivering a barrage of shells toward the beaches. Debris, sand, and jungle foliage spiraled fifty feet into the air along with exploding palm trees.

Soon nothing else could be detected, except one earth-shattering explosion after another. Sharp cracking shells and the boom of aerial bombs surrounded the APDs everywhere, in front of them on Tulagi and behind them over Guadalcanal. The Raiders had already responded to the loudspeaker order—"All Marines get below"—where they and the sailors could still feel the repercussions vibrating the ship's hull.

The invasion bombardment from ships and bombing runs from planes continued, and in the dawning light, huge billowing balls of smoke and fire could be seen dotting all the islands. Six float planes flew over spotting targets, and forty-four dive bombers came in from the carriers *Saratoga* and *Enterprise*. The barrage marked the commencement of the Solomon Islands campaign, "the longest, bloodiest, and bitterest campaign in naval history."[*]

Slowly, according to schedule, all four APDs—the *Gregory*, commanded by Harry, the *Little*, commanded by Gus Lofberg, and the *Colhoun* and *McKean*—approached Tulagi's beach, code name Beach Blue. In perfect order they halted beyond the coral reefs that encircle the island. At 6:50 a.m., Harry ordered "Drop Anchor"; shortly afterwards, Admiral Turner gave the principal command: "Land the landing force." Game on.

Immediately, the decks were engulfed in controlled chaos as Higgins boats and other landing craft began to be lowered into the water. Raiders formed up by company, strapped with heavy packs, hand grenades, bandoliers of ammo, faces covered with black and dark green camouflage paint, and long strips of canvas hanging from their helmets.

Harry came down from the bridge wing for a while to shake hands with the company commanders and give well-wishes to as many of the departing warriors as he could. "Go get 'em!" he said in hushed tones as they hurried past him. "Godspeed!" Many of the other sailors were extending the same wishes to these Raiders they all had come to not just like but enjoy. Ensign Bob Adrian had formed many friendships among the Raiders, who had finally forgiven him for coming on board and occupying yet another smidgen of space. Motor mechanic Oswald Austin told several that he had personally shined up the Higgins boats just for them.

From his vantage point on the bridge wing, Commander Harry Bauer had a bird's-eye view of the Raiders' amphibious landing. By 0800, 1st Marine Raiders—Edson's Raiders—were clambering down the swinging cargo nets into the Higgins boats. High rolling waves

---

[*]   Newcomb, Richard, *The Battle of Savo Island*, New York: Henry Holt, 60.

generated by the bombing concussions and coral reefs banged the boats into the ships' sides. Lacking something to hold on to once inside the boats, men braced themselves best they could against the turbulent rocking.

Each Higgins boat was operated by coxswains from the APD crews. Other sailors manned machine guns in the bows spraying the beaches with suppressing fire as their craft advanced swiftly toward the landing area.

Bauer was encouraged to see most of the boats, once loaded, making good headway, but not all. One of the boats was speeding forward when suddenly it grounded on a coral reef with a quick and jarring halt. Raiders standing inside staggered with nothing to grasp, and many were thrown to their knees.

Harry watched events unfold and whispered under his breath, "God help them! Come on guys, get up and get going!"

Raiders in the wedged boat slowly recovered and clumsily climbed over the sides and down into chin-deep water. One of the shorter men was struggling under the weight of his equipment and full cartridge belt with grenades hanging all over him. Two taller Raiders immediately rushed to their brother's aid and quickly helped him gain his footing.

As the second wave was debarking and headed toward shore, Harry thought he heard rifle fire coming from the direction of the *Little*. He hesitated for several minutes, then called his friend, the commanding officer of the ship.

"Gus, Harry here," said Bauer into the handset. "Thought I heard rifle fire over there."

"You did," returned Lt. Commander Gus Lofberg. "Unfortunately, somebody's rifle discharged while they were loading into the boats and killed one of the Marines. Otherwise, from what I can tell, looks like the landing is going nearly unopposed."

"Looks that way to me, too," said Harry, "though I'm sure it won't be that way indefinitely."

Harry was correct in his assessment. The landing on Tulagi was met without opposition. The only death during the invasion at the beaches was, in fact, the unfortunate death of the Marine from a rifle discharging accidentally as he boarded a landing craft.

During this second wave heading to shore, Ensign Bob Adrian had joined the commander on the landing outside the bridge. Both cheered as they saw the shorter Raider lifted up to more secure footing. Then, he hoisted his rifle above his head like all the others and resumed his struggle wading to shore.

Just a few minutes later, Harry spied Col. Merritt Edson climbing into a Higgins boat from the *Little*, which was anchored on the starboard side of the *Gregory*. "There's Colonel Edson himself," he said to Adrian.

"How do you know that's him, Sir?" queried the young ensign.

"I can tell by his small stature and his helmet. See how it's bobbing? His head is a bit small, and his helmet always looks two sizes too big! But don't let that fool you—he's tough as nails—the Japs will have their hands full with 'Red Mike' and his Raiders. You can count on that!" From even the limited amount of time Harry had spent with the "ol' man," he quickly realized why he had been selected for this assignment.

Harry watched Edson enter the boat, where several of his command group were already on board. "I'm sure he's about to pop to get to shore with his men," thought Harry. The next scene unfolded while Harry watched with empathy, but also with a degree of amusement. Raider Peatross describes the event in his book *Bless 'em All*:

> Deftly maneuvering the Higgins boat away from the *Little*, the coxswain increased engine speed and headed his craft for the beach, seemingly happy at the chance to show off his boat-handling skills for the colonel. After motoring only a few hundred yards from the ship, however, the engine stalled and to the great embarrassment of the young coxswain, the boat began to flounder. Since all coxswains had very specific orders to return directly to their own ship or another specifically designated, passing boats ignored the frantic waving

from Edson and members of his group in their once "free" boat. Ironically the only boat specifically designated to cope with such problems was itself a problem, helplessly wallowing and completely at the mercy of the sea.

Finally, after much frantic waving and not a few strongly worded threats from Edson, an empty boat came alongside, took the Raiders aboard, and landed him—much later than scheduled.*

Harry watched the scene unfold and couldn't help but shake his head with a commiserating chuckle to himself. "That poor guy is in for it!" he thought. "And for that to happen to Edson, of all people! Yikes!" Harry learned later that Edson quickly caught up with his men and all was well.

The landings on Guadalcanal also went surprisingly smoothly. The presumption was that Edson's Raiders would be back aboard the APDs by nightfall. All the APDs, transports, and other ships in the channel remained on high alert through the day, even though the invasion on both islands began in such an encouraging manner. Troops were solidly ashore, and Japanese initial response had been amazingly light—at least initially.

But stunned enemy troops on both islands promptly rallied, especially on Tulagi. Once the Japanese special forces shook off their initial shock, fierce and bloody fighting ensued. During the next 24–36 hours, things changed dramatically, especially on Tulagi and beyond what anybody could have ever imagined, tragically on the waters in the channel.

Though resistance wasn't initially a problem, even on this first day a major problem was, in fact, emerging, especially on Guadalcanal. Beaches were jammed with off-loaded supplies, food, and ammunition. By afternoon, over one hundred transport craft were in place to unload, and another fifty ships were waiting off-shore for a parking spot.

---

* Peatross, Oscar, *Bless 'em All*, 110.

The supply convoy commander, Captain Lawrence F. Reifsnider, was determined to do his job, which was to deliver all his cargo ashore. He assumed that the Marines would then haul the loads inland.

Marines found that notion completely quaint, since they were highly skilled as warriors and not stevedores. They retrieved their rifles and marched off into the jungles.

Admiral Turner, realizing that an impasse existed on the beaches, ordered the unloading halted. This would prove to be most unfortunate in the weeks ahead.

As evening closed in on August 7, it became apparent to the APDs that the Raiders would not likely be returning to them by supper as previously thought. Harry conferred with Gus and the other APD commanders and their destroyer screen captains. They all had heard the news that Edson's Raiders had eventually encountered stiff resistance, incurring many casualties, and two of his primary leaders had been severely wounded. Nonetheless, the Raiders were making steady headway.

That evening, Harry met with all his officers in the Wardroom for a quick overview of the day's activities. Everyone looked weary, but cautiously optimistic.

"The landing itself went well. So far so good—Thank all of your men for a splendid job. As you've probably heard, Col. Edson says his guys have now run into some very stiff resistance . . . but if anybody can get the job done, it's those Raiders! Our thoughts and prayers are with our brothers out there tonight. Now, try to catch a little sleep. Tomorrow will come soon enough."

As Harry was returning to his cabin, he met French in the passageway.

"Evenin' Cap'n," French saluted his commander. "I've already turned down your bunk—Can I fetch you somethin' from the mess, a sandwich or anything?"

"No, thank you on the sandwich, French. But if you've got some ice cream somewhere, I'd love a bowl," said Harry. It was the first time in many hours he felt he could breathe easy.

"I'll do better than that. I'll get you some chocolate cake. Thought I'd have it for them Raiders if they'd returned tonight."

"No, they won't be coming to us tonight. They've run into some pretty tough opposition. But I'll eat some in their honor," said Harry, grinning sheepishly.

The Lt. Commander liked the spunky young man nearly half his age. They had established an easy and amicable relationship: Harry was good-natured and respectful of the people around him, and French was easygoing as long as he wasn't pushed into a corner. But, as different as the two men were, there seemed to be something similar in their personalities, something intangible, but definitive, nonetheless. Recognizable or not, they had hit it off.

After eating his big bowl of ice cream and cake, Harry lay down on his bunk. The day had gone well. He prayed for those on the islands and those on his ship, then slept solidly for a few hours. The Lt. Commander would need the rest; the disaster of the next two days was only a brief time away.

CHAPTER 17

Disaster Begins: August 8–9, 1942

"The purpose in a man's heart is like deep water, but a man of understanding will draw it out." Proverbs 20:5

Harry Bauer jerked awake around 3:30 the morning of August 8. The tension and workload of the past several days had been heavy, and he had been in a deep sleep for only four hours, yet he felt hyped. Adrenaline is an amazing thing—it had already kicked in once more.

Through the night, ships of the fleet had steamed back and forth around Savo Island and in the channel off Guadalcanal. As Richard Newcomb says in his seminal work, *The Battle of Savo Island*, "All night long they steamed in perfect formation, and no one interfered with anyone else, and everyone grew accustomed to the idea that this was working very smoothly." [*]

But they all knew—every commander, every sailor, every cook and mess attendant—that the Japanese would respond at some point, in some way. "When?" was the question.

The first warning actually had occurred on the previous day during the landings. A coast-watcher named Paul Edward Mason, high in the mountains of Bougainville, a large island some 420 miles north of Guadalcanal, had spotted Japanese planes flying south. "Twenty-four torpedo bombers headed yours," his keyed radio message read.

---

[*] Newcomb, Richard, *The Battle of Savo Island*, New York: Henry Holt, 1961, 70.

Fighters were launched from carriers *Enterprise* and *Saratoga*, and in a spirited, high-altitude engagement, the Japanese lost some fourteen bombers and two fighters while the Americans lost eleven fighters and a dive bomber. The remaining Japanese planes turned and headed north again, as the Marine forces continued landing on the islands, relatively unopposed.

Harry and the other APDs held their positions off Tulagi in the early hours of August 8 to see how things might develop. They didn't have long to wait. By mid-morning on the 8th a second coast-watcher, Jack Read, also on Bougainville, keyed out: "Forty-five dive bombers going southeast." At this point all transports ceased unloading *en masse* and got under way. Cruisers and destroyers steamed into a screening formation, and fighter planes were summoned once more.

All the APD commanders urgently ordered their crews alerted. "'Boats,'" said Bauer forcefully to his boatswain's mate standing nearby on the bridge, "Sound General Quarters!" Immediately, the young sailor leaned to the bridge's 1MC and blew into it a quick, shrill whistle that penetrated the entire ship, followed by the order: "General Quarters— General Quarters—*All hands man your battle stations!*" It was the start of a tense, busy day.

As Japanese bombers arrived, artillery firefights from the fleet erupted. In the melee, seventeen enemy bombers were shot down but not before one managed to penetrate the smoke, crashing into a transport, the USS *George F. Elliot,* sitting not far from the APDs. A crippled Japanese bomber, maneuvering through smoke and fire, appeared to target the *Elliot* in the final moments. The plane crashed into the starboard davit, exploding at the bridge. The ship burned continuously through the day and night from a ruptured oil tank.

It was all too close for comfort. At some point during the day, the decision was made to reposition the APDs, *Gregory, Little, Colhoun,* and *McKean,* into the relative safety of Tulagi Harbor.

Located between the little island of Tulagi and a larger island called Florida Island to the northeast, was a small but spectacular harbor, deep and well-protected. Once inside, the passageway into its waters could be easily defended by destroyers guarding its narrow entrance. The other end of the harbor was too small and shallow for a ship to navigate.

Harry welcomed the news, since he knew it would be easier to load any critically wounded Raiders from the back side of Tulagi. It would turn out to be a fortuitous decision for more reasons than this.

The APDs headed south, then around the tip of Tulagi. Sailors on deck stared across the water wondering how Edson's Raiders were faring now. Ensign Bob Adrian joined LCDR Bauer on the bridge.

"Do you suppose the Raiders are making progress?" Bob asked his commander.

"I've heard Maj. Ken Bailey has been seriously wounded and others—many casualties," returned Bauer, soberly. Bailey would later be awarded the Medal of Honor for his heroics on Guadalcanal during the Battle of Edson's Bloody Ridge.* Harry knew the Raiders would be sending wounded to them as soon as they could get them to the shoreline. Then his crew would drive landing craft in to retrieve them.

At the end of the harrowing day, Admiral Frank Jack Fletcher sent word at 6:07 p.m. that he was leaving the area with his carriers, the *Enterprise*, the *Saratoga*, and the *Wasp*. So far, he had been able to keep them hidden away from the Japanese air raids in a secret location. Now, however, after the widespread intensity of aerial bombing on August 8, he felt it wise to withdraw from the region altogether. Along with these ships, the strongest part of the fleet sailed away also: a battleship, six heavy cruisers, and sixteen destroyers. This left the remaining forty or so ships without air cover.

And . . . there had been no sighting of Japanese ships headed their way. Admiral Fletcher felt the decision based on all these facts was sound. In addition, a cloudy, misty, black night was falling. No one expected

---

* For more information on the Battle of Bloody Ridge, also known as Edson's Ridge, see Appendices.

any more air attacks, or for that matter, any attacks at all by air and certainly not by sea.

It was unfortunate that what Col. Merritt Edson, who commanded 1st Raider Battalion, knew about the Japanese—that they were particularly skilled and actually relished assaults in the dead of night—couldn't be extrapolated and applied to sea engagements. That same night on Tulagi, Edson's Raiders were being initiated with the screaming, often sheer suicidal attacks by Japanese soldiers who came out of the blackness, howling and screeching like apparitions, wave after wave.

Wisely and mercifully, Edson had prepared his Raiders for these brutal nighttime battles. Col. Evans Carlson had also educated his 2nd Raider Battalion concerning the same technique. Both men, having served in China before WWII, had seen for themselves the Japanese fondness of nighttime fighting and had seen them firsthand employing the technique repeatedly to their distinct advantage against the Chinese.

But the US Navy had not experienced this. And when night fell on August 8 and all ships in Guadalcanal waters had been at "General Quarters" since daybreak due to the frequent air strikes, there was a communal sense of relief—really a pervasive belief that nightfall would bring their beleaguered crews some respite for a few hours. There certainly would be no air raids now that deep blackness safely sealed them inside the waters of Savo Sound and Sealark Channel.

All was quiet.

Close to midnight on August 8, Lt J.G. Russell E. Walton was preparing to turn over the watch on the destroyer, USS *Robert Talbot*. The ship was patrolling slowly in an area just southeast of Savo Island.

Suddenly, he was shocked to hear in the darkness a solitary low-flying plane displaying a flashing light, then watched as it passed right above him. All sailors who were on deck saw it also. An urgent message was transmitted to other ships. Some received it and waited for orders, others received it and brushed it off as some lone spotter, still others either didn't receive it, or received it and ignored it altogether.

Of the tragic events that then unfolded in the dead of blackness, historian Newcomb says of those midnight hours: "This night surely must mark the death of innocence, the last stand of the credo: 'If you don't know what it is, assume it's friendly.' All the ship commanders waited, and from the top, there came—nothing."[*]

However, there was one who was not waiting or resting, who stood as alert and razor-focused on the black waters as a wary and cunning fox carefully inching toward a coop full of sleeping hens: fifty-four-year-old Admiral Gunichi Mikawa, commander of the Japanese Eighth Fleet.

The sharp-eyed, seasoned warrior had led his division forces at Pearl Harbor and at Midway—a success at one, a stinging defeat at the other. On this night, however, he led a task force of two battleships, seven cruisers, and several destroyers, with his flag aboard the heavy cruiser, *Chokai.* His drawn face was chiseled with solid determination. As he gripped the splinter shield on the bridge of his ship, Mikawa stared into the darkness as his task force glided silently past Savo Island, which he had craftily used to hide behind so radar wouldn't spot his ships.

Quietly, the ships steamed through the narrow seven-mile-wide slot between Savo Island and Guadalcanal. Mikawa passed the sleeping USS *Blue*, thinking it nearly unbelievable they had rolled by completely undetected.

The hungry fox was now in the midst of the hen house. And at 1:33 a.m., he issued the battle order: "All ships attack."

Just a few hours earlier, General Archie Vandegrift and other sub-ordinate commanders had been summoned for a conference with Admiral Kelly Turner on the USS *McCawley* the evening of August 8. During the meeting the admiral had informed all of them that since the carriers had left, his transports would have no air cover. Therefore, he planned to pull them all out the following morning at 6:00 a.m.

Vandegrift listened with growing concern at this news. His Marines were already operating with minimal supplies—really on

---

[*]   Newcomb, Richard, *The Battle of Savo Island*, 95.

shoestrings—since the force had been summoned out ahead of what he understood the predicted date would be. In the meeting Vandegrift concluded, correctly, this would leave his forces in a "most alarming" predicament.

In an effort to assuage the general, Admiral Turner noted he intended to continue unloading supplies all through the night in an attempt to get as much as possible ashore. Little did Turner realize the enormous chaos about to erupt in the channel.

The conference adjourned shortly before midnight, and a very concerned Vandegrift returned to the minelayer, USS *Southmore,* that had ferried him over to the meeting. Once Vandgrift was back aboard, the ship began its journey over to the relative safety of Tulagi Harbor where the APDs and screen destroyers were moored.

He had just collapsed into a chair in the tiny wardroom to contemplate this disturbing development for his Marines. Being left stranded with shortages of supplies was a critically unfortunate state of affairs he had not counted on.

Suddenly, interrupting his deep concentration, a frantic message blared over the intercom:

"Commodore, you better get up here! All hell's broken loose!"

CHAPTER 18

Alone in the Solomons—
August 9–10, 1942

"The words of a man's mouth are deep waters; the fountain of wisdom is a bubbling brook." Proverbs 18:4

Harry Bauer and everyone on the APDs, along with their destroyer screen escort in the relative safety of Tulagi Harbor, were attempting to recuperate from the exhausting previous forty-eight hours of the Pacific War invasion. Those who could, tried to get a little shuteye. Without any warning, Harry was suddenly stunned awake by the abrupt explosions he could hear resounding from the channel in the distance on the other side of Tulagi Island. With a single command issued by Japanese Admiral Mikawa, Savo Sound and Sealark Channel had erupted into deadly chaos. Simultaneously, with sound and vicious fury, torpedoes hissed through the waters, cannons fired, and ear-shattering blasts blanketed the channel. Everywhere at once fires, smoke, blinding lights, and the terrified screams of agony and burning men pervaded the air.

Afterwards, APDs anchored in the relative safety of Tulagi Harbor with their destroyer screen to await further developments.

What transpired during the next minutes and hours would come to be known as the worst US naval disaster in history. Before dawn's early light on August 9, 1942, more than 1,200 men had been killed and over 800 had been severely wounded, most of these within a timespan of less than an hour. Of ships in the Pacific Fleet, four heavy cruisers were sunk in the darkness: HMAS *Canberra* (Australian), the USS *Quincy*, the USS

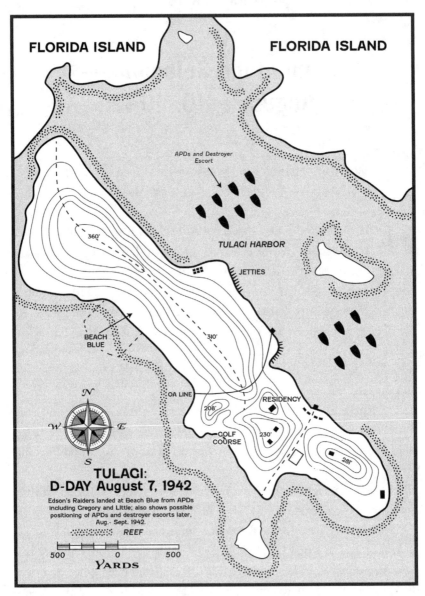

FLORIDA ISLAND

FLORIDA ISLAND

APDs and Destroyer
Escort

360'

TULAGI HARBOR

JETTIES

BEACH
BLUE

310'

OA LINE

RESIDENCY

208'

GOLF
COURSE

230'

281'

TULAGI:
D-DAY August 7, 1942

Edson's Raiders landed at Beach Blue from APDs
including Gregory and Little; also shows possible
positioning of APDs and destroyer escorts later,
Aug.- Sept. 1942.

REEF

500   0   500
YARDS

Tulagi Island showing Beach Blue, landing site for Edson's Raiders on D-Day.

Vincennes, and the USS *Astoria*. In addition, one heavy cruiser and two destroyers were badly damaged.*

As morning dawned, the full extent of what had occurred during the dark hours of night became apparent. The only saving grace was that the Japanese ships had fled before daylight. Had they remained, they might have finished off the remaining US ships, in particular the ones with limited offensive weapons like the APDs. The surviving officers and crews were deeply shaken at the magnitude of the losses.

News of the tragic events quickly reached Pearl Harbor. When the message was delivered to Admiral Nimitz, without a word he picked up his firing pistol and headed for the firing range, a practice he performed daily around the same time. However, on the day he learned of the disaster in the waters around Savo Island, it's said that he could be heard firing long and with rapid intensity. When he finally returned to his office, he was grim-faced but back under control, his stoic demeanor restored.

Harry was in a total state of disbelief as to the messages he was receiving through their radio circuits. He urgently contacted Gus on the *Little*. Soon all the APD commanders had messaged back and forth as well as communicating with their escort destroyers in the harbor. It wasn't long before catastrophic reports began filtering across their radios, each one worse than the previous report. Harry kept his crew apprised of information as he received it, but he knew the announcements were devastating to hear.

Thankfully, however, that same day there was some good news to report.

As soon as he received the victorious message from Col. Edson about the Raiders' progress on Tulagi, he shared it with his men. The respect and fondness of his crew for these lively warriors engendered most of them to refer to these Marines as "*Our* Raiders."

---

* Hoffman, John A., *Once a Legend: "Red Mike" Edson of the Marine Raiders*, Novato, CA: Presidio, 1994, 182.

He switched on the 1MC and announced the good news. "On the *Gregory*, this is the captain. You will be glad to know that headquarters received this message from Col. Edson last night: 'Tulagi Island is secure.'"

A loud, resonating cheer arose from the *Gregory*. It was indeed welcome good news. In the coming hours, the wounded being brought aboard would evidence proof, however, of what the cost had been.

The attack by the Japanese fleet during the night of August 8–9 had halted the unloading of all supplies. By nightfall of August 9 Admiral Turner ordered every ship to get underway. Most would return to Noumea; some, like the APDs, would sail to Espiritu Santo.

With the transports would go most of the "Marines' food, all heavy engineering equipment, except one small bulldozer, and most of the sandbags and barbed wire needed for the construction of defensive positions. Except for the Japanese, who controlled the sea and the air, the 1st Marine Division and the Raiders were essentially alone in the southern Solomons."[*]

In his memoirs, Captain Bob Adrian, who had been the young ensign to make his entrance on the *Gregory* swinging from a boatswain's chair accompanied by loud protests from Raiders, remembered these days vividly. One day in particular, August 10, was one he would never forget as long as he lived:

> Our Raiders secured Tulagi on the 3rd day, with high casualties. Their brothers in the Guadalcanal invasion were pinned down after taking their first objective, the partially finished air field—re-named Henderson Field after the heroics of a Marine pilot at Midway who was killed during the battle.
>
> General Vandegrift directed that we land any of our remaining "fightable" Raiders to help the Guadalcanal force, after we secured Tulagi. We did this early on the 4th day and

---

[*]　Peatross, *Bless 'em All*, 45.

picked up all the wounded that needed to be evacuated—all Doctors and their equipment to support the Marine landing were still on the transports that had been evacuated to Espiritu Santo. The other APDs—*Little, Colhoun,* and *McKean*—were ordered to do the same. We headed across the channel and could still see catastrophic evidence of the disaster the night before.

As we were loading the wounded, I was called to the bridge by the captain.*

As Bob entered the bridge, he reported directly to Bauer, who looked noticeably haggard but calm.

The USS *Gregory* APD-3 with the USS *Little* in lower left corner. Known as "the little ships that could," they are shown here practicing amphibious landings with 1st Marine Raider Battalion, South Pacific, 1942. Photo courtesy of Navy Military Archives.

---

*   Robert Adrian memoirs.

"Bob, we've got a bad situation. One of the Marine company leaders was brought aboard in a restraint jacket to keep him from attempting to commit suicide. Apparently, last night in a heavy melee firefight with the Japs—in all the confusion—he identified a group firing close by as Japanese and ordered his company to take them under fire. They turned out to be another Marine company—a number of them were killed: a 'blue-on-blue' fiasco. When he discovered his mistake, he broke down and had to be restrained from taking his own life. I'm putting you in charge of him until we get to Espiritu—we can turn him over to a doc there."

Harry paused a moment and took a deep breath.

"Keep talking to him, Bob—do what you can. But whatever you do, don't leave him for a moment—he's really in a bad way." Harry placed his hand on the young ensign's shoulder.

"Aye, aye, Sir," Bob said and headed for the Wardroom where two sailors were guarding the distraught officer. Bob hesitated before entering the room—he had no idea what to expect.

As he walked through the door, he saw the Marine sitting on the edge of a chair with a sailor stationed on either side. The Marine was hunched over in the straitjacket and rocking rapidly back and forth, staring down at the floor. The sailors came to attention when they saw Bob, who quickly brushed off any formalities.

"Stand at ease. How's he doing?" he asked his shipmates.

"Not good, Sir. We've had to prevent him from banging his head against the table—one time he tried to get out the door when somebody opened it. Hopefully, he'll just wear out eventually."

"The Skipper sent me down here to relieve you, but I'll have you stick around outside the door. I might need you," said Bob, taking care to talk in quiet tones to the two guards.

"Will do, Sir," said one of them. "We'll be right outside the door. Call if you need us." They exited the Wardroom, and Bob pulled up a chair next to the Marine. He wasn't certain that the man even realized he was present beside him.

"Hey, Sir." Bob started off very quietly. "I'm Ensign Bob Adrian. Can you tell me your name?"

The traumatized Marine sat perfectly still for a long time. Finally, the man looked up at Bob—the first time he had even acknowledged his presence. The officer's face was completely contorted with anguish, red and puffy from crying, his mouth hanging open with his lips stretched backwards exposing almost all his teeth, like a wounded animal. His breathing was labored, coming in short gasps.

"I killed them," he groaned. "God help me, I killed them!" He kept repeating those words over and over, gradually raising his voice until he was almost screeching. He kept trying to stand; Bob would place his hands on the guy's shoulders, forcing him to stay seated.

"Look—it was a mistake. You thought they were Japs—in the jungle, at night—nobody could see. You didn't mean for them to be killed." Bob was trembling now himself.

"It doesn't matter—I'm responsible for their deaths. They were great guys—they'll never go home. They're dead because of me. Kill me, kill me—give me a pistol, please, please!" He began rocking back and forth again, violently.

Bob continued to try to console him with words, restraining him when necessary. But there was no consolation for the sorrowing Marine leader.

At one point, there was a knock on the wardroom door. The sobbing Marine had exhausted himself for a moment, and Bob quickly stepped to answer. It was French from the galley.

"Skipper sent me to see if you might want somethin', some fresh coffee maybe. He told me 'bout that trouble—poor fella," said the mess attendant, peering around at the confined man seated in a chair.

"Yeah—he's out of his head. French, I sure could go with a cup of coffee. I don't dare leave him—he tries to get out of the room whenever the door opens. He's settled down a bit right now, but as soon as he rouses, I'm sure he'll be after it again."

"I'll getcha a nice hot mugful—comin' right up. Do you think he might take a bite to eat?" asked French.

"I don't think so, but you might bring coffee—I'll see what I can do." Bob thought at least he could try.

"Boy, that's too bad 'bout what happened to them men—and him too." French turned and left for the galley, shaking his head.

The hours slowly ticked on as the *Gregory* sailed for Espiritu with their cargo full of wounded souls, those outwardly and those inwardly. In later years, Bob Adrian said the journey that day, trying to console a man who was inconsolable, were the longest hours of his life. Word of the event spread throughout the crew—everyone felt empathy for the broken Marine.

From Harry Bauer to Charles Jackson French, the ship's crew suffered the weight of the past several days. It was depressing to think of all the men who had lost their lives or been wounded, most of those very seriously. Tension had been steady, never letting up. And always, in the back of everyone's mind was the fact that these little ships, the APDs which had become beloved by the Raiders, were so vulnerable. No APD sailor, however, entertained a thought that this significant endangerment could hold them back from completing their mission—their vital role of aiding "our" Raiders.

CHAPTER 19

New Duty in Hell's Waters: August 10–15, 1942

"The Lord is in your midst, a mighty one to save." Zephaniah 3:17

The *Gregory* continued her course away from the Solomons at top speed of 28 knots. Once they arrived in Espiritu Santo, the wounded were transported ashore. There, temporary medical tents had been set up a short distance from the harbor, and a small building to one side accommodated the most severely wounded. Bob Adrian's charge was one of the first to be evacuated, placed in the hands of a doctor and two corpsmen. Harry stood on the bridge wing watching. He wondered if the Marine officer would ever recover from what had happened.

"I can't imagine anything much worse," he thought.

Dropping anchor in the spectacular tropical waters that would inspire James Michener's classic book, *Tales from the South Pacific*, assuaged the senses. The lovely island was a welcome sight. But more importantly, these waters were safe—by comparison anyway—and the APD skippers and crews could relax for a few hours, get some rest, regroup. Harry called to Gus on the *Little* to see how he was doing.

"Gus, come over to the *Gregory* if you get a chance today," Harry suggested. Gus accepted the invite and the two men visited together for a couple of hours. It was therapeutic for both of them.

They talked about the amphibious landings on Tulagi—successfully landing 300 of Edson's Raiders and their subsequent securing of the island. Then the totally unexpected, tragic events during the night of August 8. Both men were deeply concerned about having to leave the

Marines on both sides of the channel stranded. But the commanders knew if anyone could make the most of the situation, it would be Edson's exceptional warriors stuck on Tulagi.

"Red Mike will have them eating anything they can get their hands on," laughed Gus.

The conversation, however, quickly turned to what would be next for the APDs—the "Green Dragons" as the Raiders fondly called them.

"We're expendable, you know," said Harry.

"Especially now," said Gus. "The fellows on the 'Canal are having a helluva time holding on to Henderson Field. Reports say the Japs are sending in 5,000 troops by way of Tokyo Express every night."

"We've got to get some supplies to all of them," said Bauer. "And they could use Edson's forces."

Both men were in full agreement. After a moment of silent contemplation, their conversation turned to home briefly, each one giving the other a quick update of their families.

Finally, Gus rose to return to the *Little*. It had been a wonderfully pleasurable couple of hours of camaraderie for both of them.

"Take care of yourself, Harry," said the tall, slender Swede.

"Same to you, Gus." Harry imagined his friend probably looked more like his ancestor, Leif Erikson, at that moment than he ever had in his life.

The two men shook hands heartily, accompanied by a warm grasp at each other's shoulders. They had shared many life experiences together: classmates at the Academy, faculty members at the same time, and both had applied for Naval aviation and not passed—Harry due to eyesight issues. As for Gus, his academic knowledge was nearly perfect, but his flight instructors said, "No one tries harder but, he has no air sense." The two men had married within weeks of one another, and each had a daughter born the same year, their girls now seven years old. They had shared many things together so far in their lives. Now they shared the immutable bonds of war. The visit had been just what each needed.

It had been a whirlwind ten days since the US invasion forces had landed in the Solomon Islands. To Charles Jackson French, however, like to so many that participated in this the largest amphibious landing up to that point in US history, it seemed more like ten years instead of ten days. When LCDR Bauer had told the crew before they left San Diego that they were headed into the thick of things, he wasn't kidding. It was clear that even though there had been success in some of the operations, there had been failure in others—with fierce fighting and devastating losses. That gripping realization plus the tension of being at General Quarters for extended periods of time had worn down everyone.

French and the other mess attendants took the news of the USS *Vincennes* particularly hard. All of her twenty-four stewards and mess attendants were African Americans. The ship was one of the heavy cruisers that went down during the battle of Savo Island. Several of the *Gregory* messmates knew sailors who had been on the *Vincennes* or one of the other ships. They knew immediately that the likelihood of some of them being killed was almost a certainty. Their fears were confirmed when, in later months, the body count listed nine mess attendants who had perished during the dark, early morning hours of August 9.

The young man from Arkansas stood on the deck while "the smoking lamp was lit," looking out over the brilliant turquoise waters to the settlement of Espiritu Santo in the New Hebrides Islands. Beautiful sandy beaches, waving palm trees, and gentle waves seemed to beg him to join them; he wished he could just dive in and get lost swimming in this tropical paradise.

As the young man's second tour of duty unfolded, it contrasted totally from his first enlistment in the Navy. Of course, the war was the most obvious difference. But there were other things. He had met some men—actually a couple of officers—that he really liked and who returned friendliness and respect, beginning with the most important, LCDR Harry Bauer. French felt at ease around him and actually enjoyed working for him. The young officer, Ensign Bob Adrian, was another—Adrian had always been cordial to the steward, didn't talk down to him. Then there was the motor mechanic from the Coast Guard, Oswald Spencer Austin, who most everyone called "O.S." for short, pronounced as two separate letters—French got along with him, too.

"Maybe," he thought, "it's because we're all at war and we all know we gotta depend on each other." French thought about all the sailors—most of them were okay, even that Alabama guy, although he still didn't believe French could swim. When the two passed each other on the ship, there was always wisecracking between them. The mess attendant flicked his cigarette stub off into the ocean. It was edging toward supper hour—time to get things going in the galley.

For most of the month of August, the Marines on Guadalcanal, Tulagi, Gavutu, and Tanambogo endured a lack of all supplies, including rations. As Peatross explains, "It was a final act of desperation to press the APDs of Transport Division 12 into cargo service as transports, initially to deliver supplies essential for the operation of the airfield."[*]

This decision came from the top shortly after the *Gregory* had arrived in Espiritu. The ships of the invasion task force had reverted back to being directly under Admiral Ray Spruance, who had succeeded Admiral "Bull" Halsey in the Pacific. After conferring with CINCPAC (Commander in Chief Pacific Fleet Headquarters), it was agreed to do whatever possible to shuttle as many supplies as feasible back to the Marines on Guadalcanal. The Raiders would need to stay on Tulagi for finalizing the mop-up of their operation there, but primarily because it remained too risky to carry them across the channel to Guadalcanal safely. They would need to stay in place for several more days, obtaining food however possible. But the sooner they could be transported to Guadalcanal the better—their help in securing that island would be welcomed, in reality desperately needed. Vandegrift began counting the days until he could get the Raiders as safely as achievable across the channel.

In the meantime, all the APDs, including the *Gregory*, would now fulfill a different role—the task of blockade runners. The ships would

---

[*]   Peatross, Oscar, *Bless 'em All*, 45.

slip silently back into the waters from hell—only at night in hopes of not being detected—loaded with life-giving supplies for the Marines.

The news that they would be returning to the 'Canal brought the immediacy of war sharply back into focus. LCDR Bauer informed the crew. They began to prepare the ship for her revised duties. Bob Adrian, along with mechanic O.S. Austin, were indispensable in getting the *Gregory* ready for her first nighttime run on August 15. Adrian recorded after the war some of the alterations made to the *Gregory* for her new task: blockade running.

> Since our APDs were expendable, and we would probably never get our Raider Companies back because of their need in the desperate struggle the Marines were having in holding their position in control of Henderson Field on Guadalcanal, we were directed to remove the bunks from the Raider's Compartment and use it for storage and re-supply of the Guadalcanal Force (and bring back their wounded) by high speed runs made by us ("up the slot" it was called) between Espiritu Santo and Guadalcanal—always arriving at night when we couldn't be seen by Japanese aircraft who frequently patrolled the area.
>
> With the first landing of the Marines, they had a company of SeaBees (12 Bulldozers) to get the field operational, which they did under constant fire from the Japs. In about the second week of the operation, two squadrons of Marine fighter-bombers from Midway landed and took up daily scouting patrols. They probably saved the whole operation from being overrun by Japanese—they spotted (and sank) 6 Japanese Troop (LST Tps) ships enroute to land on Northern Guadalcanal to reinforce their comrades who were close to pushing our invasion back into the sea.[*]

---

[*]   Robert Adrian's personal journals.

The first run "up the slot" was made on August 15.

When the *Gregory* steamed away on August 14 from Espiritu headed for Guadalcanal, Harry felt like they were riding a floating tinder box due to their cargo, primarily fuel. Even the most naive sailor could see their situation. He had correctly determined that the APDs were expendable. To keep his officers apprised of their mission, he had held several meetings in the Wardroom. None of the crew lacked the will to be blockade runners—they just recognized the potential for disaster.

Finally, after about sixteen hours, the *Gregory* steamed slowly into the southern end of the channel under the cover of darkness, back into the waters of hell. The night was silky smooth, under a waxing moon with about 17 percent illumination. Scattered clouds added to their cover. But the *Gregory*'s crew knew that every sound would echo over the water; any necessary commands or messages were delivered in hushed tones. They all knew the drill.

Extra lookouts were posted and kept diligent watch. Attacks could come unexpectedly from air, sea, or beneath them; submarines had been reported patrolling the channel. As they neared the area where they would rendezvous with Marines on Guadalcanal, one of the lookouts thought he spotted some flashes of light across the water. Harry joined him on the bridge wing, as did two others.

"Keep watching," Harry quietly relayed to the lookouts. After several minutes of peering into the darkness and seeing nothing, he quietly said to the helmsman, "Steady as we go."

Within a brief period of time, the dark form of their predetermined rendezvous point just south of Lunga Point could be identified in the distance. Making as little noise as possible, the Higgins boats loaded with supplies, ammo, and fuel headed to shore. O.S. Austin, coxswain of the lead boat, slid behind the wheel of the Higgins boat and carefully maneuvered toward shore.

O.S. could make out several figures standing at the water's edge waiting for them. "Sure hope those guys are ours, Sir," he said to the young landing craft officer, Lt. Heinrich Heine Jr.

"No kidding," Heine said.

About that time, their craft dragged slightly across crunching coral but thankfully didn't get hung up. Then, a thud into sand, and an unmistakable voice with a pure American accent said, "Where the hell have you guys been? All we've had to eat out here's maggots and stinking rice!"

The boat was suddenly surrounded by several "raggedy-ass Marines" who were overjoyed to see incoming of anything other than bombs and shells. They made quick work of unloading the much-needed supplies. After the boat emptied, they reloaded it with several wounded to be taken back to Espiritu Santo. O.S. headed the craft back to the waiting *Gregory*, thankful not to see anyone in a straitjacket.

Here the *Gregory* and the *Little* deliver men and supplies to Guadalcanal. The APDs played a vital role during WWII in the Solomon Islands. Photo courtesy of the Navy Military Archives.

Harry Bauer stood on the bridge overseeing the operation.

"Well, one nighttime blockade run in the books," he said to Bob Adrian who watched with him along with other lookouts. "Let's get back to Espiritu! Flank speed!"

"Aye, aye, Skipper," said the lieutenant and called the order down to the boiler room. In return, a stout voice could be heard. "Ahead Flank!" and very quickly the "little ship that could" was going as fast as it could go, leaving hell's waters behind in her wake.*

---

* Interviews with Don Austin, son of Oswald Austin.

CHAPTER 20

Blockade Running:
August 16–30, 1942

"Be strong and courageous. Do not fear or be in dread of them, for it is the Lord your God who goes with you . . ."
Deuteronomy 31:6

Over the next several days, beginning in mid-August, these beloved destroyer-transports—the APDs—would carry a total of 400 drums of aviation gasoline, 32 drums of lubricants, 282 bombs, and CUB-1, an aviation unit consisting of a Seabee airfield construction team with five officers and 118 enlisted men. Bob Adrian explains the mechanics of what the APDs did:

> August 16 was the first of four runs we made up the slot (the other 2 APDs would follow in successive days), and other than supplies of munition and food for the Marines, we had our decks loaded with Drums of Aviation fuel for the Marines' flight operations. These drums would be lashed together by the Boatswain's mates with heavy hemp rope, and the Marines would meet up with us offshore with a large tank lighter (LVT), and received the end of the rope and fasten it to the back of the lighter, taking a strain on the line and the boatswains aboard would roll off the ship each barrel as the lighter took a strain on its section and pulled them all ashore.[*]

---

[*] Robert Adrian's personal journals.

After the initial, nerve-racking nighttime run, everyone on the *Gregory* breathed a sigh of relief once they were headed back to Espiritu. Their respite was short-lived, however. As soon as the *Gregory* could be reloaded with more supplies, they turned around and headed back to Guadalcanal. One Marine on the 'Canal had said during their first nightly run with supplies, "This food will last us about three days!" He was thinking of the 18,000+ Marines who had invaded the Solomons and who needed to be fed. The Solomon Islands campaign didn't come to be nicknamed "Operation Shoestring" for nothing.

The nighttime runs were always accompanied by challenges. Reports from the channel indicated that every night Japanese surface ships shelled the islands. On land, Marines spent many sleepless nights in their foxholes while the Cactus Air Force did their best to fend off the bombing and shelling. Troops began calling the firefights their "nightly pyrotechnic show and entertainment." But no one sensed the danger in these dark, hostile waters as did these converted destroyers—the APDs—and their faithful crews.

After the 1st Marine Raider Battalion, Edson's Raiders, had been on Tulagi for three weeks, the decision was finally reached that it was time to transfer them over to Guadalcanal, dangerous as the crossing might be. Despite the obstacles, it was a welcome mission for the *Gregory*.

Harry Bauer relayed the news to his crew. "On the *Gregory*, this is the Captain. I have some good news! We are going to see our Raider brothers again. We've been assigned the task of taking them from Tulagi over to the 'Canal. It'll be great to welcome them back!"

French and others in the galley vowed to have some special treats on the *Gregory* for their Raiders once they boarded. All of them looked forward to seeing the warriors who had been so successful on Tulagi—they couldn't wait to hear the stories of defeating the enemy, yet they well knew the price that had been paid to secure the island.

French was determined to find some sweet canned fruit, cookies, crackers, maybe even some ice cream. If he couldn't obtain it on shore, perhaps he could barter with one of the other ships anchored at Espiritu.

Before they left for this critical run, Harry reminded everyone they might wish to compose a note to loved ones. Mail would be picked up and taken back to the States on a ship leaving the following day. "Don't forget to write home," he spoke over the ship's 1MC, with a warm tease in his voice.

Harry had already composed a long letter to Jackie and little Mimi. He was finally able to give her his location and disclose what they were doing. These were details that sailors had not been allowed to share before the invasion and for a couple of weeks afterwards. But now, at the end of August 1942, newspapers were already reporting some of the activities in the Solomon Islands. It wouldn't be long before most newspapers and magazines stateside were carrying stories of the Marines, the Raiders, and the actions of ships in Guadalcanal. What had once been an unknown region of the world would soon become a household name.

But this letter also carried some other thoughts. Harry had been reminiscing about the days when he and Jackie first met in the yearbook workroom at Chattanooga High School. He was the editor-in-chief and she was in charge of producing articles for the annual. He had liked her immediately, the dark-haired beauty that she was with a wonderful smile, friendly, and full of laughter. Their temperaments were very similar—they had hit it off from the beginning. He told her how much he missed her and how he looked forward to seeing her again. "Give a hug to Mimi for me. My love forever, H." It was his usual simple closing. He sealed the letter, held it for a moment, and handed it to the sailor collecting mail in a large sack to be delivered to the ship headed back to the States the following day. During the war, it usually took about a month—sometimes longer—for mail to reach back home from deep in the Pacific.

Once more, the APDs departed the safety of Espiritu and steamed toward the dangerous waters off Guadalcanal. This time, however, it was a mission they all anticipated with excitement—to be reunited with their friends, the victorious warriors who had been on Tulagi nearly three weeks. The Raiders returned to the *Gregory*, *Little*, *McKean*, and *Colhoun* as conquerors, killing all but three of the Tulagi defenders. They embarked on the APDs, welcomed aboard with cheers and backslaps. Mess attendant French and the other mess deck attendants made sure bottomless cups of coffee poured forth from the galley along with cookies and chocolate sheet cake cut into bite-sized portions.

Many had souvenirs that they shared with their sailor buddies. Maps, flags, a couple of bugles, and even a golf club were among the spoils of war. Edson's Raiders had discovered a small golf course on Tulagi, complete with a clubhouse. Several bags of clubs and other golfing paraphernalia were among the things that made their way back to the *Gregory*. Executive officer Lt. Col. Sam Griffith told Harry, "See! I liberated some golf clubs!" Needless to say, the swabbies were ecstatic over the shared spoils of war.

The mood onboard was celebratory, yet laced with a sobering, grim reality. In the battles, thirty-eight Raiders had been killed and fifty-five wounded. The *Gregory*'s crew rejoiced in seeing their Raiders again while regretting the ones left behind. At the same time, the sailors speculated what their next steps would be once they reached the shores of Guadalcanal. Harry stood on the bridge watching carefully as his ship steamed across the channel which held the potential for danger with every rotation of their screws.

Tulagi was now officially behind the 1st Marine Raiders but had forged a lasting impression. Years later, in 1957, 1st Raider John "Black Jack" Salmon wrote, "I can still smell that moldy barley, and I remember our great friends on the gallant APDs and those finest ones we left behind."

"Dog" Company of Edson's Raiders spent their time crossing the channel on the *Colhoun* (APD-2), reacquainting themselves with many of her crew and viewing the dark form of Guadalcanal coming into sharper focus.

"Wonder what we'll find over there?" mused one Raider to another standing at the railings along *Colhoun*'s deck. Little did they know that in just thirteen days they would be involved in a ferocious engagement that would forever bear the name of their commander, Merritt Edson, and be compared to landmark victories in Marine Corps annals: the Battle of Edson's Bloody Ridge on Guadalcanal.* But for now, they were just eager to reach the shore.

Not far from the long, narrow strip of white sand that outlines most of the island of Guadalcanal, the Raiders began disembarking.

Lt. Heine and Oswald Austin as coxswain headed their Higgins boat crammed with Raiders toward shore. All of a sudden, their boat came to a jarring halt, lodged on a bed of rock. The Raiders immediately began scrambling over the sides. Heine and Oswald had no choice but to join.

"Come on," said one of the Raiders to Oswald as he headed toward the beach. "Stick with us and see what war is really about," he laughed, as he watched Heine and Oswald crawl, somewhat awkwardly, over the side into the surf and scramble behind the men now making their way inland.

Following quickly, the two sailors ducked into the treeline behind the Raiders. With their .45s drawn, they had only penetrated the dense jungle a few yards when the Raider on point halted abruptly. Signals were given and everyone dropped to their knees.

Suddenly, a shot rang out. The next thing the astonished sailors observed was a large bundle of something tumbling down through the large palm fronds and thick foliage. It turned out to be a Japanese soldier who had been hiding in the trees. A sharp-eyed Raider sniper had spotted movement and fired. As the Raiders were examining the soldier, there were shots from the beach behind them. Since Oswald and Heine were at the rear of the group, they were first to arrive back at the beach.

When they emerged from the jungle, they saw a Raider struggling with a Japanese pilot who had evidently just been shot down and was attempting to come ashore. Heine and Oswald fired shots into the air, which helped subdue the melee.

As the other Raiders surrounded their second incursion of the day, they also secured him and then searched his pockets. In one they found

---

* See Appendix B: Brief Overview of the Battle of Bloody Ridge.

several Japanese coins. Turning to Heine and Oswald, the Raider laughed and tossed the coins to the sailors. "Here you go! We're paying you for our ride here!"

Only thirty minutes ashore and Lt. Heine and coxswain Austin had experienced a sniper event—and helped capture an enemy pilot![*]

In the following days after securing the area, the Raiders went inland a short distance and established their bivouac in the middle of a picturesque but deserted coconut plantation. The tall, regal coconut palms formed interesting outdoor housing which the Raiders quickly nicknamed the Coconut Grove, in honor of the ritzy, well-known area on Biscayne Bay, Florida, a favorite gathering place for millionaires, artists, writers, and musicians.

However, the crossing on August 30, 1942, would not remain uneventful for the ships themselves. Later that same afternoon, the Japanese staged a bombing raid with a flight of eighteen bombers at 15,000 feet. It was a dreary, dark day with fog and mist. The USS *Colhoun* (APD-2) was patrolling after debarking the Raiders when the Japanese bombers spotted her. Raider Corporal Maxwell Miller had waded to the beach in the last group of Raiders to debark the *Colhoun*, when he heard the air raid alarm.

Official designation for these high-altitude Japanese bombers was the Navy Type 1 Attack bomber. But the Allies called them "Betty" bombers; the Japanese pilots who flew them used the nickname "Hamaki," Japanese for "cigar," suggested by the plane's rounded cigar-shaped fuselage. Later reports stated that on this overcast day, there was a small break in the heavy clouds, and one of the "Betty" bombers made an almost unbelievable direct hit on the *Colhoun* amidship. Some said it was the most accurate drop from the highest altitude during the entire war.

"Everyone took off for cover in the tree line along the shore," Miller remembered later. "About halfway there I heard the explosions and spun

---

[*]   Interviews with Don Austin, son of Oswald Austin.

around. *Colhoun* had been hit dead center. Her bow and stern were lifted up in the air, out of the water, and she began sinking rapidly . . . It was a horrifying sight."

Another Raider, Private First Class Ben Quintana, remembered the tragedy as well. "As I hit the beach, I dove behind the first tree I came to, and as I looked back out to sea, all I could see was the bow of the *Colhoun* settling into the water."

The first direct hit wrecked her boats and aft davits and ignited a diesel fire. Just moments later, during the second wave of bombers, several more hits on the starboard side brought down the foremast, exploding two 20mm guns and one four-inch gun off the ship; the engineering spaces were damaged in total. Two more direct hits killed all the sailors in the deck house.

The Raiders, helpless to lend aid to their friends, were devastated at what they were watching from shore. Immediately, they set about for the next eighteen hours helping to rescue as many burned and oil-soaked survivors as possible.*

Harry saw the flames in the distance but wasn't certain which ship it was until he got a keyed radio message. "The *Colhoun*'s been hit—she's going down. Lots of crew lost. Will keep you posted. Keep heading south out of the channel." Harry immediately maneuvered his ship south, knowing the catastrophe happening with the *Colhoun*—and also knowing that he was forced to abandon two of his crew on Guadalcanal, Lt. Heinrich Heine and coxswain Oswald Austin. He prayed Heine and Oswald were okay on land. "Well, at least they're with Raiders."

For Harry Bauer and his crew, as with those shipmates on the *Little* and *McKean*, the sinking of the *Colhoun* was gut-wrenching. They had all been so delighted to welcome aboard the Raider heroes of Tulagi, to

---

* Alexander, Joseph, *Edson's Raiders: The 1st Marine Raider Battalion in WWII*, Annapolis, MD: Naval Institute Press 2001, 111; Maxwell Miller to John Sweeney, March 10, 1934; Ben Quintana to *Dope Sheet* editor, Irv Reynolds, August 13, 1991.

hear the stories, mostly glorious. To witness the return of these brave warriors to their ship was completely uplifting. The sailors could see firsthand what their own contributions to the mission had accomplished: they felt they, too, had accomplished something important . . . and indeed they had.

But now, to hear of the sinking of one of their sister ships was a gut-punch. They didn't know the exact number of crew that were killed or wounded—they didn't have to know. The ship had received several direct hits. The bombs had ripped the *Colhoun* apart, and she sank within two minutes. This could only result in one thing—many casualties. And, in fact, later when body counts were assessed, nearly half of the *Colhoun's* crew, fifty-one sailors, had been killed and eighteen seriously wounded.[*]

A state of gloom settled over the entire *Gregory* at such heart-breaking news. Harry felt it too. Since high-altitude Japanese bombers were in the area, the APDs were advised to withdraw from the immediate channel off Guadalcanal. They steamed south about sixty miles or so past the southern end of the 'Canal and waited.

However, within a day or two, the APDs would be recalled for yet another dangerous transport mission in the ferocious waters. This time, to carry a group from 1st Raider Battalion under command of the battalion's executive officer, Lieutenant Colonel Sam Griffith, from Guadalcanal to Savo Island. They had been tapped for a highly dangerous scouting expedition to rout out potential Japanese soldiers brought in by the Tokyo Express—a treacherous assignment for both the "brave little ships" and the Marine Raiders.

---

[*]   Ibid, 111.

CHAPTER 21

Japanese Coins:
August 31–September 4, 1942

"The cords of death encompassed me; the torrents of destruction assailed me." Psalm 18:4

Colonel "Red Mike" Edson, commanding officer for 1st Marine Raiders Battalion, had only been on Guadalcanal an hour before he began planning a reconnaissance patrol. After consulting with Vandegrift, it was decided that Lt. Col. Sam Griffith would lead a company of Raiders over to Savo Island. Reports were coming in that a group of Japanese soldiers had been dropped off on the island during a Tokyo Express nightly run to establish a radio station. Griffith and his men would scout out and eliminate the communications center, hopefully lessening the number of incidents in the channel.

Positioned some sixty or so miles south of Guadalcanal, Harry was still awaiting specific orders as to when to reenter the channel waters. Bob Adrian remembered in later years: "On this our fourth trip up the slot from the south around September 3–4, the Marines were so short on fuel that our sister ship, the *Little*, was ordered to accompany us with her topside also covered with barrels of aviation gas."[*]

Once the two ships made the journey back to Guadalcanal, the fuel barrels were unloaded. It was during this run that Harry and Gus Lofberg on the *Little* learned about "Red Mike" Edson's plans for a Raider patrol to scout Savo Island. Subsequently, after unloading fuel,

---

[*] Robert Adrian's personal journals.

they would then embark Griffith, along with Companies "A" and "B" of Raiders, and deliver them to the shores of Savo within the following day or two. As important as the new mission was, Harry was also eager to find out what had happened to Heine and Oswald—hoping they were unharmed—and how they had made out on their unique and unexpected excursion on Guadalcanal with their Raider pals.

As soon as possible, Lt. Col. Sam Griffith began embarking the *Gregory* and the *Little* with his Raiders. Among them were, indeed, the missing sailors. When Harry saw the young Lieutenant Heinrich Heine and his coxswain, Oswald Austin, coming back aboard the *Gregory*, he yelled down from the bridge wing.

"Well, it's about time the deserters came back!" he said, laughing at his shipmates but glad to see they were safe and none the worse for the experience.

"Sir, have we got a story to tell you!" yelled Oswald back to his commander.

"Can't wait to hear it—tell me after we get these Raiders delivered to Savo," said Harry, clasping his hands together in a victory sign.

After the *Gregory* approached the small island, not far from Cape Esperance on the northern tip of Guadalcanal, Lieutenant Heine and Oswald readied themselves once again to make the short trip to Savo Island in one of the Higgins boats.

"Maybe we'll get lucky this time and not get stuck again!" said Heine to Oswald, with a laugh.

"Yes sir," replied the coxswain. They both agreed they had had enough shore excitement to last them a while. And they couldn't wait to share their story with the Skipper.

They watched as Raiders clambered into the landing craft to head to shore. Fortunately, the lieutenant's and coxswain's luck held, and they landed their Raiders not far from the shores of Savo Island without running into rock.

Maj. Gen. Oscar Peatross, former Marine Raider, describes the events of September 4:

"On September 4 Lieutenant Colonel Sam Griffith and companies 'A' and 'B' embarked the *Gregory* and *Little* and sailed to Savo where they landed and searched the island thoroughly for Japanese who had been reported to be there. None was found, and the Raiders re-embarked, returned to Guadalcanal, and began unloading. As the unloading was nearing completion, Griffith received orders from Colonel Edson to remain aboard the APDs for a raid of Tasimboko on the following day. However, the order had arrived too late, and the Raiders finished unloading.* Then, instead of retiring to Tulagi, the APDs took up patrol stations offshore." †

After Oswald helped with delivering the Raiders back to Guadalcanal and had secured the Higgins boat in its davit, he decided to head to the bridge to see LCDR Bauer. It was around 9:00 p.m., and the *Gregory* and *Little* were slowly steaming in a continuous circuit about four to six miles off Guadalcanal's shores near Lunga Point.

Harry, as well as Gus over on the *Little*, had received reports of a submarine sighting around Cape Esperance. They placed their crews on high alert and planned to patrol throughout the evening. Besides, the night was inky black with a low-hanging mist that blurred any forms in the distance. It would mean picking their way through the thick darkness in a dangerous channel to reach their anchorage over by Tulagi Harbor.

But primarily, the two commanders were concerned about the Raiders they had just deposited on the beaches of Guadalcanal. Dubbed the Tokyo Express, Japanese transports usually accompanied by subs prowled like a pack of hungry wolves along the shore's edge, usually beginning around midnight. Anything the *Gregory* and the *Little* could do to alert their Raiders on shore of an attack would be time well spent. Harry had just peered out into the darkness once more from the bridge

---

* For more information see Appendix B for what happens next to "Red Mike" Edson's 1st Marine Raiders.

† Peatross, Oscar, *Bless 'em All*, 91

wing when he looked up to see young Oswald standing at the bridge entry.

"Come in, O.S.—tell me about this adventure you and Heine had on shore! I'm guessing the Raiders showed you a thing or two!" Harry always seemed to be in good humor and enjoyed mixing it up a little with the crew.

"Yes, Sir, they sure did," said Oswald, who proceeded to relay the adventure. "Well, Sir, those Raiders went ashore, and after Lieutenant Heine and I realized we couldn't get that Higgins boat off the rocks by ourselves, we had no other choice but to follow those Marines ashore. They were making pretty good progress when a shot rang out. The lieutenant and I were behind the Raiders and everybody hits the dirt. I'm telling you Sir, that jungle's so thick you can't see more than two feet!"

"That's what I hear," said Bauer. "Makes you glad you're on a ship, right?"

"Yessir," laughed Oswald. "Well, me and the lieutenant, we drew our 45s and there we were right in it. One of the Raider snipers thought he saw something up in one of them trees, and he fired. Next thing I know, I see this bundle come bouncing down through the limbs and palm fronds and landed almost in the middle of us. It was a Jap, and he was alive—bummed up some, the Raider had nicked him, but definitely alive! The guys searched him, then got him tied up to take him to camp."

Oswald stopped to take a breath.

"Well, that was an adventure!" chuckled Bauer.

"No, wait—that's only the half of it," O.S. continued. "Next thing we knew, we heard shouts coming from the beach back behind us—a lot of commotion—and we all rushed back to the beach to see what was happening. Since lieutenant and I were at the back of the group, we got there before the others—we saw a Japanese pilot who'd been shot down trying to get ashore and one of the Raiders in a fight with 'im. Lieutenant and I rushed down, fired some shots in the air, and helped subdue this Jap. The Raiders tied him up, searched him and found these on 'im—gave two or three to each of us."

Oswald plunged his fist deep down into a pocket of his dungarees. Pulling out his hand, he looked up at Harry with a large grin. "They gave 'em to me—Japanese POW war souvenirs!" Oswald opened his fingers to reveal several Japanese yen.

"Well, well, O.S., you've got yourself a real Guadalcanal campaign keepsake!" said Harry, opening his eyes wide and grinning. Harry had always enjoyed the company of the eager, young Coast Guardsman who was self-assured with great mechanical skills. Oswald had told him the story of how he had met his wife, Grace, when stationed in New Smyrna Beach, Florida, and when as a teenager he had flushed a herd of wild cattle from the brush in the outer banks of North Carolina. Harry had teased O.S., calling him a "cattle baron."

"Now, you're a tycoon of the Orient! Be sure and save those for Grace!" said Harry.

They had a good time joking about the events, ruing the fact that the Navy didn't have opportunities to collect souvenirs like the Marine Raiders did. It was a welcome moment of levity during what had been a tense, draining month of blockade runs in the black, deadly nighttime waters off Guadalcanal.

About that time, Lieutenant Bob Adrian joined them on the bridge. Bob had bridge watch as assistant Officer of the Deck. He heard the last part of O.S.'s story and wanted to see the coins himself. Oswald proudly pulled them out again. Bob listened to Oswald relate his Raider adventure story once more, shaking his head and choking back a laugh— "Guess that'll teach you to get stuck on rocks!"

Harry greeted Adrian and updated him on their situation. "Reports say there has been a submarine spotted the past two nights—used its surface gun to bombard the Marines' position ashore. We'll keep a close watch tonight, Bob. The *Little* is patrolling with us at about 2,000 yards out."

"Aye, aye, Skipper," replied Adrian. After so many months together and multiple intense missions, he felt completely at ease with Lt. Com. Bauer and completely confident in his leadership—as did the entire crew.

It was just past midnight. Harry had just returned to his position of overseeing things from the bridge after a brief break in the Wardroom. Those now on watch were also getting into position, including Adrian. The dense night was as dark and gloomy as any they had seen during these days in the channel off Guadalcanal. The thirty-seven-year-old commander thought about all the things that had happened since the invasion of the Solomon Islands over the past month—some successes, some abject failures. In fact, it would take the Navy two more months to publicly release information about the debacle around Savo Island. The loss of so many planes and ships, including the USS *Colhoun,* an APD sister ship of both the *Gregory* and the *Little,* were onerous events to digest. In the murky darkness, he could barely make out the waters constantly rocking his ship beneath him, but he knew how much life they had claimed.

While he stood on the bridge, along with Bob Adrian and Oswald Austin, peering into the darkness, another warrior made ready to search the dark night. A pilot revved up his Black Cat, a PBY painted matte black and used for nighttime reconnaissance patrols. He was headed out to look for enemy ships in the channel in efforts to stave off another attack on Marines hunkered down along the shores and in the jungles. At 0056 on September 5, not long after the pilot was airborne, he saw gun flashes toward Henderson Field and immediately dropped five flares to illuminate what he thought was the enemy. Midnight in hell's waters, however, showed no mercy.

Part II

Living Beyond Ironbottom Sound

How do waters become sacred? By human sacrament as when a priest blesses with it, or a prodigal plunges for cleansing, or a parent seeks holiness for their newborn? Most assuredly, all gracious reasons . . . But there is a sacredness that only comes from sacrifice—the sacrifice of human life offered up freely for others on the altar of selflessness. That's how the waters of Ironbottom Sound became sacred—and will remain so into eternity.

—author unknown

CHAPTER 22

Spring 1993

"The Lord will keep your going out and your coming in from this time forth and forever more." Psalm 121:8

I t was late in the day of what had been a lovely spring afternoon in Annapolis. Having recently retired from his position at Annapolis Banking and Trust, Bob Adrian continued to serve as vice chairman of the board. He had worked most of the day in his basement office reviewing paperwork for several Navy widows who lived in the area. Bob was someone they all knew, respected, and trusted, and he helped them in an advisory capacity with their financial affairs.

Now, it was time for some fresh air. The retired captain pulled out his bicycle and headed in the direction of the Academy cemetery next to College Creek, not far from where the Severn River flows into the Chesapeake Bay. The view out over the waters was one of his favorite spots.

As he pedaled along, he thoroughly enjoyed the wind in his face. It always reminded him of being on the bridge wing of a ship and feeling the ocean's sharp, salty air swirling all around him.

It only took him a few minutes to travel from his house down King George Street to Maryland Avenue, then through the pedestrian gate into the Yard. Before long, he was on the bridge crossing over Dorsey Creek and decided to pull over to the side of the road. Bob stared toward the river. Clouds were gathering, and the wind was picking up. The day was darkening.

There was something about the weather on this particular afternoon that reminded him of that incredibly dark night in Sealark Channel over fifty years ago—the body of water that came to be known as Ironbottom Sound. Once clouds had rolled in on that day in the Solomons and darkness had closed in all around them, the *Gregory* began picking its way through the channel transporting Marine Raiders to Guadalcanal. It was one of the blackest nights Bob had ever seen—perfect for an undetected disembarking of troops.

As he straddled his bike near the Severn, the waters began responding to the wind—the waves had turned angry. In the distance he could see two majestic sailboats under full sail making a beeline for the safety of Annapolis's harbor. He decided it best to turn around and head home.

On the way back to his house in the gathering gloom that had descended so quickly over the Naval Academy, he continued to think about that dreadful night over fifty years ago on the *Gregory*. What transpired during those brutal hours was forged upon his memory. How could he ever forget what had happened, the death and destruction, the enormous sacrifices of so many?

A sudden flash of lightning directly overhead lit up the darkness, followed almost immediately by a deafening crack of thunder. Bob felt an unexpected stab of acute anxiety—the flash of blinding light had ignited an all too familiar memory. "Damn!" he muttered to himself, "Flank Speed!" He quickly ramped up his bicycle and headed for the basement wardroom at home: his own safe harbor.

CHAPTER 23

Night of Infernal Darkness: September 5, 1942

"Greater love has no one than this, that someone lay down his life for his friends." John 15:13

Shortly after midnight, three Japanese destroyers, in what had become a regular routine throughout the month of August, unloaded troops in the Cape Esperance area on the northern part of Guadalcanal. Dubbed the Tokyo Express, the ships sometimes delivered as many as 5,000 troops in the gloomy darkness. On this unusually bleak night, the destroyers, after debarking their troops, sailed down the coast of Guadalcanal a few thousand yards and began shelling Henderson Field.

Gus Lofberg on the *Little*, along with his shipmates on watch, saw the light flashes and immediately assumed it was the submarine they had been alerted about. Before he and Transport Division Commander Hugh W. Hadley could decide whether to attempt a hit-and-run attack or withdraw completely, a Navy reconnaissance pilot dropped his flares in the vicinity of the APDs. As a result, both the *Gregory* and the *Little* were clearly silhouetted against the blackness.

Bob Adrian, standing beside Bauer, was one of the *Gregory*'s crew to witness the flares lighting up the darkness. He recalls those horrific moments:

"It was about 1:00 a.m. when we were lit up by several flares dropped above us from a Black Cat PBY who had apparently also been called in to look for the sub with his surface radar and had picked us up and dropped the flares. I happened to be on the bridge watch at that time as

Assistant Officer of the Watch. With a quick look towards the shore, I and the Captain saw three Jap destroyers steaming in column and in opposite direction than we were, close in to the beach to obviously bombard our Marines' position. They saw us under the flares and shifted their guns on us rather than on the shore. Captain Bauer immediately ordered, 'RIGHT FULL RUDDER. FLANK SPEED AHEAD' to try getting away from the incoming Jap destroyers. I stood facing the rear bulkhead of the bridge with the sound powered telephone to the engine room, relaying the Captain's FLANK SPEED orders . . ."*

Commander Gus Lofberg on the *Little* immediately ordered his ship to commence firing, although he knew without doubt that his three four-inch guns and a handful of 20mm guns would be no match against the far more powerful, modern five-inch guns of the Japanese destroyers. Gus also knew one more important fact—his ship could not outrun the destroyers, which were closer to the *Little* than to the *Gregory*.

Maj. General Oscar Peatross described what ensued during the next catastrophic minutes:

> The Japanese bracketed the *Little* with their third salvo and their fourth was dead on target. One shot smashed into the steering engine room jamming the rudder, another hit the aft field tanks spewing burning fuel all over, and a third knocked out the aft 4-inch gun. As the Japanese continued to lay it on, Lofberg decided that the only chance to save his stricken ship would be to beach her. She was already virtually dead in the water, however, and could not be maneuvered. Reluctantly, Commander Lofberg gave the order to "Abandon ship!", but before he could follow his crew over the side, a shell struck the bridge, killing him and Division Commander Hadley.†

---

* Robert Adrian's personal journals.
† Peatross, Oscar, *Bless 'em All*, 112.

At the same time, the *Gregory* was also in dire straits. When the Japanese destroyers saw both ships silhouetted against the sky by the flares, they began firing simultaneously at the vessels. Oswald and the commander looked out across the water and saw the enemy ships bearing down. (Most accounts identify these Japanese destroyers as the *Yudachi*, the *Hatsuyuki*, and the *Murakumo*. There is also an account that four ships were seen on radar from the *Little*, the fourth believed to have been a Japanese cruiser or perhaps a submarine.)

Within the next few seconds, an ear-splitting explosion erupted on the bridge. A direct hit tore the bridge apart, and both Bauer and Oswald fell forward some twenty feet or more to the deck below. At the same time, the boiler and galley deckhouse were totally destroyed in a hail of fire. Landing on a portion of the deck not yet engulfed in flames, Bauer and the coxswain were stunned, having suffered tremendous damage to their legs. At the same time, Bob Adrian, who had also been on the bridge, was unconscious for several minutes. When he came to, he could feel the ship turning over.

"I had no sooner relayed the Captain's 'flank speed' orders than we took a direct hit to the bridge—about a five to six-inch shell on the port side. It knocked me out and when I came to, the ship was turning over to starboard and I just floated off into the water as the ship was going down," Adrian remembered.*

The direct hit on the bridge by Japanese shelling rocked the entire ship. Sailors from all over the *Gregory* were racing topside to leap off the ship. Almost immediately after the first horrific explosion, the *Gregory* began listing. Charles Jackson French had just lain down in his hanging bunk still warm from the previous shipmate: Raiders and crew alike crammed into the APDs accepted "hot-bunking" as a daily reality.

As explosions rocked the bunks, sleeping sailors sprang to their feet in the midst of the erupting chaos. Charles ran to the nearest ladder, emerging topside into mayhem. There were wounded men on fire, others

---

* Robert Adrian's personal journals.

screaming from shrapnel wounds, everyone frantically trying to escape the hellish environment. The sounds of men suffering and crying out were everywhere.

At that same moment, a shipmate with his back in flames ran by Charles and threw himself into the water. Then, another sailor without any clothes on, who had apparently been in the middle of taking a shower, came running past him. The seaman spread his arms and dove into the water yelling, "New construction, here I come!"

Charles took one look toward where the bridge had been just moments before and knew his naked shipmate's sentiment was correct: the *Gregory* was lost. He hesitated only a moment and jumped into the murky water. Sailors are trained to get away from a sinking ship as fast as possible to avoid being sucked down with it. But in this terrifying bedlam, he acted strictly on instinct—the instinct to survive. As he landed in the turbulent channel, he spotted a large rubber raft bobbing up and down not far off. With a few strong strokes, he reached it and pulled himself up and over the side. Several sailors were already aboard, each one gasping for breath and all of them with varying degrees of wounds.

As Bob Adrian drifted away from the *Gregory*, he knew the waters off Guadalcanal were shark infested. He later recalled what happened during the desperate moments shortly past midnight.

> I was in my Kapoc life jacket and as I floated, I could hear voices and cries in the distance—so many sharks in the area but apparently with so many sailors in the water, they never got to me, even though I had a fairly good-sized shrapnel wound in my right knee which was bleeding profusely. The first thing I did was to drop off the heavy Colt 45 pistol we had to wear at general quarters, and pulled off my class ring and put it in my pocket so it wouldn't slip off my finger as my hands withered in the salt water. I noted that my right eye felt like it was full of dirt, and my vision from the eye was

extremely poor. After a time, I heard several voices were coming from near my position, and I swam toward the voices. I came upon a life raft of the *Gregory*'s which was full of wounded sailors. Our life rafts had ropes around all sides, so I hooked my left arm around one of the ropes and tried to identify the personnel in the raft. I could only come up with French—who was not wounded—he was our 1st class black mess attendant in the Wardroom.*

Bob recognized French's Arkansas accent and called out to him. "Is that you, French?"

"Yessir—let me help get you up in the raft," replied French. French reached down with strong arms and pulled Adrian aboard. "We're in a heapa shit, Sir," yelled French over the gunfire and shelling.

"That we are," said Adrian.

Meanwhile, amidst the complete turmoil, there were dozens of sailors from the *Little* and the *Gregory*, most of them severely wounded, thrashing in the dark waters. The Japanese destroyers steamed at full speed between the two sinking ships, dropping depth charges and firing machine guns at the helpless men struggling for their lives.

The Marine Raiders stood helpless on shore, sickened at the thought of what they realized was taking place. When they heard the rapid machine gun firing and heard the screams of suffering men, they comprehended the worst. Their resolve hardened to seek reprisal for these brave men who had risked everything assisting them in their missions.

As the raft carrying French, Adrian, and other wounded shipmates drifted away from the *Gregory*, two seamen, Clarence C. Justice and Chester M. Ellis, running along the ship's edge, came across their commander. Bauer was lying in a pool of blood, both legs bent at odd angles.

"It's the Skipper!" yelled Clarence Justice. "Sir, we need to get you into the water! Here Chester, help me!" The two of them placed their

---

* Ibid.

hands under the arms of Harry Bauer to pull him quickly into the water away from the sinking ship.

Suddenly, the screams of a man yelling for help rang out not far away. Bauer roused for a moment. "That sounds like it might be Austin—go to that sailor—help him," he moaned.

"But, Sir," Justice said.

"That's an order—Go save that man," said the *Gregory*'s commander.

"Alright. We'll be back to get you! Hang in there, Sir!" They left their commander and ran back a little ways. Rounding a fiery mass, they spotted the crumpled-up coxswain, moaning and bleeding from severe wounds. Justice and Ellis floated into the water with Oswald in tow. A small rubber raft was bouncing about nearby with two other wounded men already lying inside. Together, Justice and Ellis pulled and pushed Oswald into the raft, then gave it a hefty shove away from the ship.

No sooner had they completed that rescue than machine gun bullets began peppering the water all around them. After plunging several times down into the sea, they surfaced, gasping for air, and looked around to determine where they were. The *Gregory* was now almost completely submerged. There was no returning onboard.

After being heavily shelled, the *Little* remained partially afloat for about two hours, the *Gregory* for about forty minutes, both flaming in the darkness as they went down: two brave ships crewed by brave men.

Along with his friend, Gus Lofberg, who had commanded the *Little* as long as he had commanded her sister ship, the *Gregory* and with whom he had shared so many other experiences in life, the thirty-seven-year-old seaman now shared one more: Lieutenant Commander Harry Bauer, like his friend Gus, was never seen again.

CHAPTER 24

Night of Courage

"Be gracious to me, O Lord, for I am in distress." Psalm 31:9

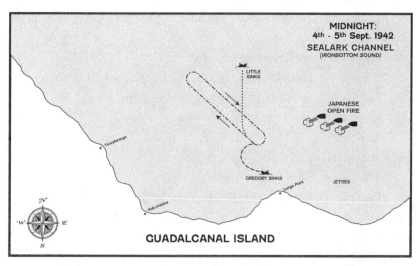

Drawing showing possible patrol positioning of the USS *Gregory* and the USS *Little* on September 4–5, 1942, after disembarking Edson's 1st Marine Raiders on Guadalcanal from Tulagi. Also shown are the possible sites of the sinking of both ships. Compare with Ensign Robert Adrian's drawing of possible sites, page 201.

Charles Jackson French leaned against the side of the raft, heaving to catch his breath. He looked around in the shadowy darkness trying to discern who was in the raft. Besides himself and Bob Adrian, he counted five others—shrapnel wounds primarily, two or three of them badly burned, all of them in dire need of immediate medical attention. As far as French could determine, however, he was the only one not injured.

"We're in a helluva mess," said Bob Adrian, who slumped beside French.

"Yessir, you sure can say that," returned French. "Those enemy cruisers whupped us. Do you think Cap'n Bauer made it?"

"I don't know. We took a direct hit to the bridge. I was turned facing the back wall relaying Skipper's orders when we were hit. I can't see anything out of my right eye—feels like it's full of dirt or something," said Adrian. His entire face was covered with cuts and beginning to swell.

About that time two sailors sloshing in the water bumped into the raft's side.

"Help! Help us!" groaned one of them.

"Gimme your hand," said French, reaching down, grasping one of the men. He pulled the sailor upwards and grabbed him by his soaked dungarees, sliding him over the raft's side.

Then he leaned over for the next man who at first appeared nonresponsive.

"Where you hurt?" asked French.

"Don't know for sure—I can't move my legs," mumbled the confused sailor whose face and arms were so blackened, burned, and covered with oil that in the darkness, French didn't recognize him at all.

"You from the *Gregory*?" asked French.

"Yeah—some of us got scorched," he said in a hoarse whisper.

French was already sliding into the water beside him. Swimming up behind the seaman, he pushed hard on his lower torso and buttocks, raising him up enough over the side for others to help pull him into the bobbing craft. Then French, using the ropes along the side, pulled himself back in.

Over the next thirty minutes or so, agonizing moments that seemed like hours, French assisted eight more floundering swabbies into the relative safety of the raft—welcome relief that brought thanks from everyone.

Most were severely injured or burned and drenched in black oil; everyone was in some degree of shock.

The raft was now perilously loaded down. No one was talking, just sitting in the heavy darkness struggling to process the sinking of the *Gregory* and the *Little*. Besides friends on their own ship, they all knew many sailors on both vessels. Several were drifting in and out of consciousness.

French sat next to Adrian, who leaned against him just to stay upright.

"French, I'm pretty sure we're drifting toward shore. We could easily land right where the enemy is!" Bob spoke in a hoarse whisper, not wishing to add any additional stress to the hurting men around him.

"Yessir—thinking that too," said French, quick to agree. "We don't wanna be caught by 'em. Heard what the enemy do to prisoners, even wounded ones—no sirree—we don't wanna get caught." French spoke with all the urgency warranted by their desperate situation.

"And we don't want to be pulled out to sea, either," added the ensign, well aware of their predicament. The channel off Guadalcanal flowed somewhat in a southerly direction headed straight into the open waters of the South Pacific, an unending expanse of deep blue.

Both men sat passively for several seconds listening to the sounds of continued gunfire in the distance, the waves slapping against the sides of their meager craft, and the continued moaning of several of the men in debilitating pain; many of them could be overheard whispering prayers.

All of a sudden, French raised himself halfway up and began pulling off his shirt, then shimmying out of his pants down to his skivvies.

"What in the hell are ya doing, French?" Adrian peered out of his one good eye at the mess attendant tearing his clothes off.

"I'm gettin' in the water. They say them sharks don't bite at naked folks—I'm counting on it, Sir! I'll tie that rope 'round me and pull us a ways from shore—only chance we got—you just watch for me and tell me where to go, Sir." The mess attendant was already down to bare skin.

"Well, alright, French. Good luck, man—You're our only hope! I'll do my best to locate Orion and make use of the stars—just remember, you've got a one-eyed navigator."

"Okay, Sir, you just tell me where to go—and I'll do my best!" French was already slipping into the dark waters with the raft's rope tied securely around his waist.

Some distance away from the craft towed by French, Oswald Austin lay on his back stretched out between two other shipmates on a small rubber raft. One man wasn't talking, but O.S. could hear his labored breathing. The other fellow was awake but grabbing at the top of his leg which was bleeding profusely.

"God, it hurts," he said. "Where were you when we got hit?" he asked Oswald, wheezing.

"On the bridge with Cap'n. We took a direct shell—I must've fallen twenty feet—landed on my knees," said Oswald.

All three men were covered in oil, and the bottom of the raft felt slippery. Oswald suddenly felt a warm sensation on his backside—he wasn't certain what it was, blood or urine.

The raft seemed to be drifting away from the noise, and before long both men on either side of him were quiet.

Oswald closed his eyes. He thought about how soft Grace's voice was—sweet Gracie. They had met when he was in the Coast Guard stationed at New Smyrna Beach, Florida. She was working in the bank, and Oswald came in wearing his surfman's uniform, very similar to a Navy officer's dress blues except for insignia. After a brief courtship, they were married in July 1939. One year later a son was born to the couple. Oswald had just learned in a letter from Grace that the toddler had taken his first steps. Oswald had only been able to spend a handful of days with him since his birth. Almost all the men he served with who had children were in the same situation.

The sounds of splashes and occasional screams and shouts seemed to be fading somewhat. He tried to adjust his legs but couldn't move them. There wasn't anywhere on his body he didn't hurt.

About one hundred yards away from Oswald's bobbing rubber boat was a struggling survivor from the *Little* who remained in the water, Chief Boatswain's Mate Suydam. He later recalled the horrors of that night:

"There were seven of us grouped in the water when one of the Jap ships came by. It picked us up with its searchlights and peppered us with machine guns. I had a Navy Lieutenant in tow and was picking the right direction to swim, referring to the position of the Big Dipper. It was the darkest night I've ever seen."[*]

At the same time the boatswain's mate realized that the officer he was pulling through the water was dead and released him to float away. He continued trying to remain afloat himself, using the Big Dipper for direction.

As the Japanese ships pressed on steaming through the waters, Oswald Austin jerked back to the present at the zipping sound of machine guns. Before he realized what was happening, a bright light swept over the waters. The next thing he knew, the water around him was peppered with bullets. He squeezed his eyes shut, not knowing for certain whether he had been hit—so numb was his body—and passed out from exhaustion, loss of blood, and sheer fright.

Farther down the dark channel, French continued to pull his raft overloaded with wounded men, now at least fifteen. He had lost track. Bob Adrian, out of his one good eye, kept directing French, making the best use of whatever stars he could see to determine direction. While trying to guide French, he tried to keep pressure on his bleeding leg. No one really thought they would live through the night.

"How'em I doing, Sir?" gasped out French to Bob Adrian. The swimmer could feel the current constantly pushing him toward land while he continued with strong strokes and paddling to direct the raft away from Guadalcanal's shoreline.

---

[*] Peatross, Oscar, *Bless 'em All*, 92.

"You're doing great, French," Adrian struggled to call back to him. It was so dark Bob could barely discern the mountainous areas of Guadalcanal looming in the distance, and then, only if the misty clouds parted slightly.

Suddenly, Adrian thought he saw a large form near the top of the water next to the raft, then it disappeared downward. Then another and another breaking the top of the water, now circling around the raft. "Damn! There are sharks all around us," said Adrian.

About that time, French suddenly spewed out a string of curse words. "Them's sharks in the water, everywhere," he called to Adrian. All of a sudden French felt a smooth, hard, suede-like object rubbing along the bottom of his feet. French was so scared, he froze. "Shit—those sharks rubbing my feet!" he yelled.

French lifted his legs straight up toward the surface of the water as best he could. His heart was pounding so hard he thought surely it would jump out of his chest. "Shit! They're everywhere!" French gasped. Several times he felt something bump him from the side but then dart away. Usually, the sharks' skin felt smooth but sometimes prickly like sandpaper if it turned suddenly while under his feet. He had never been so terrified in all his life, not even that first day he had gone way under in the turbulent waters of the Red River when he was just a boy.

French didn't speak for several minutes. Then Adrian called out to him, "French—are you okay?"

"Yessir, I think so—I guess maybe those sharks aren't hungry—guess maybe I'm more scared of what's on shore than in the water!"

Several times during the next few hours, however, the predators would return, circle the raft, then dart away. Each time, French would try to raise his feet and legs to the top of the water and, between cursing, pray they wouldn't bite him.

The long night in hell's waters continued—Adrian with his one good eye straining to help French—and the mess attendant in the water pulling and tugging a sagging raft overloaded with wounded men. He would swim and paddle until he was forced to stop, float for a while to catch his breath, then resume his mission again.

"I'm not gonna quit," thought French. "I'm not gonna quit."

CHAPTER 25

Darkest Before Dawn

"For you equipped me with strength for the battle; you made those who rise against me sink under me." 2 Samuel 22:40

During WWII in the mid-Atlantic Ocean, there existed a 300-mile deadly gap: an isolated section of water too far away for planes to reach, flying either from the eastern shores of the US or from the western runways of the European Allies. Without the vital protection of air cover, the enormous troop ships escorted by destroyers were left in an open expanse of deep Blue Water . . . virtually unprotected and vulnerable. Any ship passing through this treacherous area became ripe targets for German U-boats lurking within its dark waters like packs of hungry wolves. Thousands of troops were lost at sea before they even reached their battle destinations. So horrific was this treacherous section of the Atlantic that it became known as "The Pit" to WWII sailors and soldiers.

The waters off Guadalcanal represent a fraction of the waters of the Atlantic but would also be renamed, a devastating testament to the number of ships, planes, tanks, trucks, and materiel lost in this channel. In fact, more Americans were killed in the waters off Guadalcanal than on land. It's unclear exactly who said it first or when the channel was dubbed with its new moniker. But when it was, the new name represented its chief characteristic: Ironbottom Sound is the largest maritime gravesite in the world.[*]

---

[*] Ballard, Robert D. w/ Rick Archibald, *The Lost Ships of Guadalcanal: Exploring the Ghost Fleet of the South Pacific*, Toronto: Madison Press, 1993.

French had lost track of time. He simply had no idea how long he had been in the dark, hellish waters. Every now and then, he would see what he thought was another raft or lone swimmer in the distance, but from his limited vantage point down in the water, it was impossible to make out who or what it was with any certainty.

As the hours dragged by, the sharks seemed to disappear. "Maybe they just gave up looking for a meal around here," he thought. He guessed they had been drifting at least a couple of hours. His hands felt like wrinkled sponges, his legs were as heavy as logs. Every now and then, he would rest alongside the raft by looping one arm through its side ropes. And always he would ask Bob Adrian if he was still headed in the right direction: away from shore but not headed toward the vast expanse of the South Pacific at the southernmost end of the channel. "I'm going to tow this ol' crate in—just keep telling me if I'm goin' the right way," French continued to say.

It was during the early morning hours that French began to wonder just how much longer he could last. He had never experienced such debilitating exhaustion. He alternated swimming and pulling with floating during the darkest part of the night—just before dawn.

Neither French nor Adrian had any idea what to expect once daylight arrived. To make matters worse, French thought he felt something once more around his feet—he couldn't be sure, however. "Might just be my imagination playing tricks," he thought. He labored to come alongside the raft and hang on for a few minutes to catch his breath.

As he withdrew his arm and began swimming again, one of the men who had been passed out in the bottom of the raft for most of the night raised himself up. He was disoriented at first and looking around, he spotted Adrian.

"Where the hell are we?" he muttered.

"We're trying to stay clear of the beach," replied Adrian.

There was just a sliver of daylight now—enough for the sailor to see more than a few inches beyond his nose. He spotted someone in the water, swimming and pulling the raft.

"Who the hell's that?" asked the shipmate.

Adrian turned fully toward the wounded sailor and immediately recognized him. He was one of the southern boys from Alabama.

"That's French, you know, one of the steward's mates. He's been pulling us through the water all night, through the sharks and everything—keepin' us away from those Japs onshore. I've been using Orion to help give him directions."

"No, shit! Well, I'll be a son of a bitch—French—that colored boy can swim after all," said the sailor, shaking his head in disbelief.

As the sun broke above the horizon, French no longer required Adrian's guidance. The lieutenant slumped over in the raft and closed his eyes.

Suddenly, planes were heard overhead; the sound immediately generated anxiety among those in the raft who were cognizant. When they came into view, the desperate men realized they were friendly. Soon landing crafts appeared to pull the survivors in various places in the channel to safety.

Adrian describes their rescue from hell's waters in his memoirs:

"Early the next morning, several of the Marines' planes from Henderson Field took off and one spotted us in the water and radioed in our position. Soon thereafter, an LCP (Landing Craft Personnel) came out and picked us up. A later count figured that there were about thirty survivors from the ships in this area. I was one of two that survived the Japs' direct hit on the port side of our bridge (USS *Gregory*) where there were about twelve shipmates stationed that night: the Captain, Asst. Gunnery Officer, lookouts, signalmen, and phone talker—all killed by the direct hit on the bridge area.

"When we got ashore, the Marines put approximately twenty of us in foxholes well behind their line of engagement with the Japs. A Navy Hospital Corps (the Marines always retain several well-trained hospital corpsmen assigned to each Company) looked after our wounded. They bandaged up my knee and looked in my right eye and found out it was filled with embedded shrapnel particles or paint fragments (from the bridge bulkhead I was facing while on the phone to the engine room, when we took the hit on the bridge). He was not qualified to try to get them out and simply put a bandage over the eye.

"We soon found out the Marines were having a desperate struggle to keep Henderson Field in our possession and were taking heavy casualties."[*]

When French, still with the raft's rope tied around his waist, looked ahead at the shore, he saw several Raiders waiting for them to land. Several began to wade out into the water to assist him and the others. One Raider helped drag him through the shallow waters while others helped unload debilitated survivors. Some had to be carried on makeshift stretchers, but all were alive—and grateful for what French had done.

Once French reached the sand, however, he collapsed. The sailor from Alabama, who had argued many times with the mess attendant about his ability to swim, came up behind him. Though wounded himself, the doubter from Alabama quickly reached down to help him up.

"Man, you did a helluva job last night," he said to French, who was so tired he could barely respond. The two helped each other move farther away from the deadly waters and into shade.

The 1st Marine Raiders, along with other Marines, assisted the men from the *Gregory* in crossing the short distance back into the treeline. Eager to help their *Gregory* friends, they administered as much first aid as they could, provided water, and gave away their rations.

When the surviving sailors related all that had happened, in particular what the enemy had done—deliberately attempting to kill the wounded men in the water with machine guns—the Raiders were left in a cold rage. Many cursed vehemently and vowed retribution.

It soon became evident that most of the sailors suffered some degree of shock. Medics began arriving in the camp to help stabilize the more

---

[*] Robert Adrian's personal journals.

seriously wounded and try to get them back to the aid stations at Henderson Field.

As things were beginning to settle down a bit, several military police showed up to check out security and determine if there were any pressing needs. When they spotted French, they ordered him to come with them so they could transport him to the "colored" camp some distance away.

"Hey you, come with us!" one of the MPs shouted to French, who could barely stand. French was trying to hobble over to their jeep when one of the Raiders looked up and saw what was about to transpire.

"Wait a minute—what do you think you're doing?" the Raider said to the MP. Their racket had caught the attention of several other 1st Marine Raiders as well as the wounded *Gregory* sailors.

The MP, who now gripped French by the arm and was guiding him to the jeep, kept going. "He's not supposed to be here—he's supposed to be in the colored camp," the guard replied curtly.

By this time the *Gregory* sailor from Alabama had also heard the commotion and stepped into the scene. "No, no," he said, shaking his head vigorously, "this man ain't going nowhere—he's one of us—he's staying here!" Almost at once, those sailors from the *Gregory* who had been pulled throughout the night and could manage to walk, came over and joined the heated discussion. Others who could barely move, nevertheless, added raucous vocal support for their shipmate. Many Raiders were already standing, braced. French, who could barely hold his shoulders up from fatigue, just slumped in the middle—the MPs on one side and the sailors from the *Gregory* alongside the Raiders—on the other.

The military policemen looked at each other. They could easily identify a lost cause. "As you wish. Let's go—no use wasting our time here," they said, and climbing back into their jeep they sped off down the beach.

All during the day of September 6, 1942, men were rescued out of the water or spotted and dragged up on the beach at various locations along Guadalcanal's shoreline. Both US Navy captains had died, as had thirty-one others. Boats from the marine beachhead rescued 238 survivors that morning that included seventy severely wounded. Some were washed ashore in an isolated area where Marines on patrol accidentally stumbled upon them.*

Around mid-morning, such a patrol noticed a small raft bobbing up and down in the sand. They cautiously moved toward it, knowing it might be a trap. However, when they reached it, they discovered three men lying on its bottom. At first, they thought all three were dead. After quickly examining the men, they confirmed that two of them, the men on the outer sides, were deceased. However, the man sandwiched in the middle was still breathing—barely alive but still among the living. What clothes the unknown sailor had on were in shreds, and what fabric there was left was covered completely in oil. His name tag couldn't be discerned, and when they examined him there was no other identification.

One of the Marines carefully placed his hands in a pocket of the man's dungarees to see if perhaps anything remained there—any clues. He immediately felt something and pulled it out.

"Well, look here," he said to his buddies. They all gathered around to stare into the palm of his hand.

"How in the hell did he get those?!" said one in amazement.

There in the palm of the Marine's hand were some small objects he had extracted from the pocket of the half-dead man: three coins of the Imperial Empire of Japan.

* Hoffman, Jon, *Edson's Raiders*, 114.

CHAPTER 26

Beginning the Journey Home

"He Himself would stay, and tell the crowds good-bye, and get them started home." Mark 6:45 (TLB)

The next couple of days were a blur for most of the rescued sailors. The more seriously wounded drifted in and out of consciousness. Marine medics did what they could with what they had. Everything was in short supply.

French was one of the few who had sustained no outward injuries, but he was already experiencing difficulties nonetheless, mostly struggling to stay calm; sleeping was almost out of the question. Once he was able to regain his equilibrium and stand unaided, he still continued to fidget and pace. He had trouble just sitting. His skin looked scaly and peeled easily, the result of being in salt water for so many hours. But each day someone would come to him to express thanks for what he had done that hellacious night.

One of the men who came and talked with him introduced himself as a newspaper reporter embedded with the Raiders. He asked French to tell him about what had happened the night the *Gregory* sank and then about pulling the raft. The reporter had been told by several of the rescued men themselves that he needed to interview the mess attendant about how he had saved over a dozen of them the night their ship was sunk. French shared the event with the newspaperman, who took notes the entire time. When French had finished, the reporter just shook his head in awe.

"Man, that's quite a story," he said. "I'm going to send it to my editor back in the States—that okay with you?" he asked the mess attendant.

"Sure," French said. "Whatever you wanna do. It was something alright—we done been through hell."

"Sounds like it. The folks back home want to know what's happening out here on the 'Canal—they'll love reading about this. You're a hero!" The reporter stood up and held out his hand to shake with the mess attendant. French felt a sudden rush of pride, the good kind that accompanies well-deserved recognition for a courageous deed.

After the war correspondent left to type up his story, Bob Adrian noticed French sitting on a log not far from the foxholes. A medic had just placed a fresh bandage over Bob's right eye. The wound was too severe and complex for much else—he would have to wait until a surgeon could see him. Adrian stopped and sat down by French.

"Oh, hey, lieutenant—how ya doing?" French was delighted to see Adrian.

"Okay, I guess. My eye hurts like hell. They've given me some pain pills. How're you doing?"

"Guess okay too—jittery—my ol' hands keep shaking—can't seem to stop them," said French, staring down at his bare feet. Some of the Marines had rounded up a shirt and pants for him but were still trying to scrounge up some shoes.

"Any word on Cap'n Bauer?" French asked.

Bob just shook his head. Both were silent for several minutes.

Finally, Adrian spoke. "I heard somebody say Ellis and Justice tried to get him into the water, but he ordered them to go look after another guy yelling for help. Somebody said it may have been Oswald. Bauer ordered them to go help the man crying out. After they got him in a raft, they tried to get back to the captain and couldn't. Same thing on the *Little*. Everybody says Commander Lofberg went down too." Adrian stopped talking and took a deep breath. His face ached all over.

The two shipmates sat together quietly for many minutes; Adrian continued to take deep breaths.

This time it was French who broke the silence. "Cap'n Bauer was a good man," he said. "A good man."

"Yes, he was," Adrian said. "One of the best."

A couple days later, again during a dark night in Ironbottom Sound, two large Australian tuna fishing boats arrived and began evacuating survivors from the *Gregory* and the *Little*. About the same time, the USS *William Ward Burrows*, operating off Kukum Point, slowed after encountering all available boats picking up survivors. As the boats passed, Commander E. I. McQuiston on the *William Ward Burrows* offered to help transport wounded to Espiritu. Twenty-seven men were transferred over from the Australian fishing boats on that morning and an additional 214 later. Charles Jackson French was one of these. All ships then steamed to Espiritu Santo, where they dropped anchor in Second Channel and disembarked the APD survivors. Immediately, medics escorted them to a field hospital that had been set up in the jungle.

Once they arrived, Bob Adrian was quickly taken in for his eye to be examined by one of the surgeons. He remembers the complete exasperation all the medical personnel were experiencing:

> The doctors in Espiritu Santo were supposed be in Guadalcanal supporting the operations and were frustrated that they weren't there. All their medical supplies were buried in the cargo ship holds; they couldn't be unloaded until the Guadalcanal operation could be stabilized and the ships sent again to offload. One of the doctors went aboard a seaplane tender (for the PBYs) anchored offshore and used their shop to manufacture from copper pieces, scalpels he needed in operations on the wounded. He used one to pick out of my face and right eye all the articles embedded there, with the exception of one that was too deep in the pupil of my eye to

get to—this one particle split the vision in the eye, so I just
kept a patch on it to wait until we got back to the States.*

French was assigned a bed in the field hospital a short distance away
from surgery. Though he had no observable outward wounds, it was
immediately apparent to the doctors who examined him that he was
experiencing acute anxiety. They advised him to remain in the tent
area and to try to get some rest. French felt jittery, had great difficulty
sleeping because of nightmares, and began experiencing frequent
anxiety attacks. He was tagged by doctors with those who would be
sent on to Pearl Harbor aboard the *William Ward Burrows,* then to
the Naval Hospital in San Diego for further treatment and
observation.

Within a week after the survivors of the *Gregory* and *Little* arrived
at Espiritu, the exhausted men were delivered more crushing news. On
September 15, 1942, the USS *Wasp,* a carrier assisting Marines in the
battle for Guadalcanal, was sunk by torpedoes from a Japanese submarine. The *Wasp,* on duty about 150 miles from San Cristobal Island
in the lower Solomon Islands, took an initial three torpedoes at 14:44;
these all hit in the area of the ship's gasoline and magazine compartments. As a result, the fires on the carriers were so intense and beyond
control that the captain ordered "Abandon ship!" at 15:20 that
afternoon.

The news dismayed everyone at Espiritu, but no one took it harder
than the men who had just been through the experience of losing their
own ships. Though much smaller than a carrier, with far fewer sailors,
the men of the *Gregory* could empathize with everything that had happened to the *Wasp* and her crew.

"I'll never forget what we saw beginning that day," said Bob Adrian
in later years. He describes the utter horror of seeing the men who began
arriving at Espiritu from the *Wasp:*

---

* Robert Adrian's personal journals.

> We [began] receiving a flood of their badly burned survi-
> vors. They started coming in the next day and what an
> awful sight it was—some looked burned to a crisp—the
> only thing the doctors could do for such burns was to cover
> them with liquid wax, let it jell, and it would cut down on
> most of the pain but several would die each day and [were]
> carried away to an area designated as a cemetery—a piece
> of land that was temporarily chopped out of the jungle by
> Seabees.*

The losses were devastating. Later, they learned the final tally: 193 men
had died and 366 had been wounded.

The doctors and medics, stretched to their limit, could communicate
with all the men they were treating, at least on some level. However, there
were some that just wouldn't—or couldn't—respond. Many had no idea
where they were or even who they were. Oswald Austin, the man with
three Japanese coins in his pocket, was one of these.

When Oswald was transferred off the Australian fishing boat into
the makeshift field hospital on Espiritu, a doctor's quick examination
revealed probable extensive internal injuries with bleeding. Oswald was
unresponsive and when awake, just stared blankly into space. Since his
clothing was tattered and covered in oil, there was no hope of any positive identification. It was assumed the critically wounded man might
be a crew member either from the *Gregory* or the *Little*. Beyond that
was anybody's guess. One thing was certain—he would be among the
first evacuated on the first ship bound for the Naval Hospital in San
Diego.

Oswald, like every sailor on the *Gregory* that could not be conclu-
sively identified or accounted for, would be listed as MIA—"missing in
action." Letters with this limited information would be immediately sent

---

* Ibid.

to next of kin. Grace Austin received notification by the end of September that her husband, Oswald Austin, was missing in action.*

And so did Jackie Bauer. Since no one actually witnessed her husband's death, Harry Bauer, commander of the *Gregory*, was listed as MIA.

---

* Interviews with Don Austin, son of Oswald Austin.

CHAPTER 27

Headin' for the Chapel

"He heals the brokenhearted and binds up their wounds."
Psalm 147:3

Approximately three weeks after the men from Guadalcanal arrived at Espiritu Santo, the Navy commissioned the *Brastagi*, a Dutch passenger ship, as a troop carrier to sail eastward for San Diego Naval Hospital. Since the *Brastagi* had limited hospital care and the trip would take approximately ten days, those embarked would only be the wounded not requiring immediate and/or emergency care. It also included about thirty aviators from the *Wasp* who had escaped from their sinking carrier without injuries.

The MS *Brastagi* was a ship without a country. An enormous, old freighter, it had spent most of its years operating between the Dutch East Indies in the Pacific and its home port of Rotterdam, Holland. Once the Germans took over most of Europe including Holland, and the Japanese invaded and operated bases on most of the islands in the Pacific, the *Brastagi* had no place to call home. During WWII, the freighter was commissioned several times by the Navy for duty transporting US troops, equipment and materiel, shuttling back and forth between California, mostly San Diego Harbor, and the South Pacific.

Lieutenant Bob Adrian was one of the wounded designated to be transported back to San Diego on the MS *Brastagi*. His injured eye remained extremely painful, and medics did what they could, mainly to keep it covered with clean bandages. Every medical personnel that examined him agreed that he would require evaluation and care from an eye specialist on arrival stateside. Since those who boarded this particular ship were considered "walking wounded" rather than "severely wounded," the desire to intermingle and seek out entertainment became part and parcel of passing time.

Adrian soon discovered one of the more interesting ways some troops indulged their talents, injuries aside:

> I got a stateroom on the ship with a Marine fighter/bomber pilot named Tom Moore, an ex-cop from New York who had enlisted in 1940 in the Marine Corps flight program. Tom was one of the Marine aviators who had droned through the Midway Battle and came into Guadalcanal with the first Marine flight. His plane had been badly damaged in a bombing run on the Japs' base at Rabaul and had to make a crash landing when returning to Henderson Field. He hurt his back badly in the landing.
>
> From the time we steamed away from Espiritu, sailing without escort at about 18 knots, a perpetual crap game transpired in the ship's salon among the unwounded Navy and Marine officers. I watched it, at times, but not being a gambler, I didn't trust my unskilled dice rolling.
>
> Most of the bets were being made in IOUs—to be paid after we got our up-to-date pay when we got to San Diego. Still, there was a considerable amount of cash around the table.
>
> After about five days, one Navy lieutenant commander of the *Wasp* had cleaned out about all the bettors. One of Tom Moore's fellow Marine flyers came in our room and urged Tom to get out of his bed—if possible with his bad back—and take on the LCDR. Tom's friends said that Tom had the best reputation of crap shooting in the entire Marine Corps. None of them would go up against him.

At first Tom said he didn't have any money to get started with and if he did go, he would have to have two people help him get to the salon. I told him I had come off the *Gregory* with just a wallet with a $100 bill but I would loan him to get in the game.

He finally agreed, and said he would pay me back in San Diego, if he lost the $100, or if he came out a winner, he would split the pot with me. I said no-split—just get my $100 back to me in San Diego.

Tom was helped by his Marine friends and me down to the salon's crap table and in about two hours, he cleaned out the LCDR, tore up all the IOUs and came out with several thousand dollars!

When we got to San Diego, in about the last week in October, he wired his wife $300 worth of flowers and gave me the keys to his car (an old Chevy he had stored at the Marine Base) for me to use while he was in a recuperation state and survivor's leave in New York.

Of course the first thing I did when I got ashore in San Diego was to call my folks and Joan. They had received no word on my status router other than I was 'missing in action' with the sinking of the *Gregory*. My dad came down and spent a couple of days with me, and Joan said she would be there as soon as she could get her things together and quit her job.*

Once Bob was checked into the Naval Hospital in San Diego as a survivor of the sinking of the *Gregory*, doctors gave him a thorough physical exam. While in Espiritu the medics had filled his knee wound with sulfonamide powder, a chemical compound with antibacterial properties to prevent infection. It seemed to be healing nicely.

---

* Robert Adrian's personal journals.

The examining physician explained to Bob that in order to extract the particle blocking the vision in his right eye, it would require peeling the cornea of the eye back, then trying to extract the particle with a magnet. They had no doctors at the San Diego Naval Hospital qualified to do that sort of delicate eye surgery. Actual corneal transplants and other sophisticated eye operations were not part of protocol at that point. So the hospital requested a qualified eye surgeon from the Naval Hospital in Boston to fly to San Diego to do the operation.

Once the ophthalmic specialist arrived, he administered a light anesthetic and the operation was performed. The particle was successfully removed from Bob's eye with a magnet, the cornea sewn back into place, and a patch placed over the eye until it healed.

After Joan arrived, they picked up Tom Moore's Chevy from the Marine base and headed out to savor Bob's survivor's leave. Bob pointed the car toward Yuma, Arizona, where they could marry without any further delay. The couple had put their marriage on hold once too many times already. They wanted to make sure destiny didn't interfere again. Though it wasn't the Naval Academy chapel but rather a small "chapel" in the desert, nevertheless, they were thrilled to be together at last. Bob wore his dress uniform, Joan, a lovely tailored blue suit. Lieutenant and Mrs. Robert Nelson Adrian were now husband and wife.

Bob Adrian's eye healed nicely, thanks to the competent eye surgeon. And marrying his best friend, Joan Smith, who was truly the love of his life, made all he had endured worth it.

But war is war. Bob would have to return to duty soon enough. And there would be more challenges in the months ahead for the young lieutenant, a survivor of the sunken USS *Gregory*.

CHAPTER 28

The Celeb Swimmer

"So the Lord was with Joshua, and his fame was in all the land." Joshua 6:27

I t's hard to say exactly how the story of Charles Jackson French suddenly became so widely known in the States in such a brief period of time. Perhaps the reporter on Guadalcanal, who had interviewed French in the Raiders' Coconut Grove camp, was actually able to submit it promptly. Or perhaps sailors or Raiders may have shared what they knew about French's extraordinary feat with other newspaper editors who were in the South Pacific seeking stories of battles, heroic acts—anything of interest for readers back home anxiously awaiting news of events transpiring in the Solomon Islands. Ensign Bob Adrian was even interviewed for a radio broadcast by NBC. During that program, Bob shared the story of the "human tugboat."

Whatever the case, by the time the young mess attendant reached San Diego Naval Hospital on October 11, 1942, knowledge of his astounding deeds had preceded him. He was already on his way to becoming a celebrity in his own right.

When French was admitted, doctors immediately recognized some of the issues facing the young sailor, very similar to what so many of the young men returning from combat were battling: nightmares, tremors, the inability to focus, overwhelming emotional outbursts of either anger or sadness. He was kept quiet and isolated for a day but very quickly, due to the heavy volume of wounded arriving hourly, was soon placed in one of the large wards lined with rows and rows of beds covering nearly every square inch of floor space—some even stretched down long hallways.

French rested and took his meds. He had talked to his sister, Viola, in Omaha and his brother, Chester, who still lived in Arkansas at that time. They were ecstatic to hear his voice over the phone and know he had managed to live through the ordeal in Guadalcanal. He assured them that he had not been wounded physically—"Jus' nervous, cain't sleep," he told Viola. "I'll be catching the first train I can for Omaha, sis," said Charles. "Gotta month survivor's leave coming!"

Even before he arrived in Omaha in late October, word of his heroic deeds was being heralded around the country. A welcoming committee composed of several city dignitaries and a representative from the mayor's office met him at Burlington Station to greet the "Hero of the Solomons," as some had dubbed him. Excitement grew, and soon Viola's phone was ringing several times a day with additional requests for an interview with her famous brother.

Not long after Charles arrived at Viola's apartment, a call came in one morning with a particularly intriguing request. The officials at Creighton University, a Jesuit Catholic college that was having a football game on October 31, 1942, wished to recognize Omaha's very own war hero. Charles and Viola both were thrilled.

On a cold Saturday morning before the start of the game, rival football teams and mostly white fans in a packed stadium looked out over the field as the president of Creighton approached the microphone.

"Will you please rise. We are especially proud to introduce to you today as our special guest, Omaha's very own Charles Jackson French, who without regard for his own life, saved fifteen of his shipmates after the ship they were on, the USS *Gregory*, was torpedoed and sank in the dark waters off Guadalcanal. Without regard for his own life, Charles Jackson French pulled their raft all through the night swimming in shark-infested waters thereby keeping them safe and away from the enemy on shore. We salute him and thank him for his extraordinary courage and bravery, and their families and friends of those he saved thank him. And for the outstanding example he represents in this war, we all thank him. May God bless and keep him until peace is restored. Thank you, Charles Jackson French, we salute you!"

Charles Jackson French standing with his sister, Viola French, at the Creighton University football game on October 31, 1942. Charles was introduced as the "Hero of the Solomons" to a packed stadium. Photo courtesy of the *World Herald*, lincolnjournalstar.com.

The crowd instantly erupted into wild cheering.

Then, with his sister by his side, Charles stood at attention saluting on the football field surrounded by the college's representatives, while the Creighton University band played the national anthem. Charles was overwhelmed by all the attention, and Viola was so proud of her little brother.

The fanfare at Creighton University wouldn't be the last time the young hero from Arkansas would be recognized by organizations or publicly. He was honored at the Theodore Roosevelt American Legion Post #30, where other African American veterans took turns congratulating him with vigorous handshakes and back slaps. Then, on Armistice Day, November 11, the largest Omaha Armistice Day observance since the end of WWI, French himself led the Pledge of Allegiance to a large, mostly white crowd. They loudly cheered and applauded him afterwards.

These were exhilarating days almost beyond imagination for the young man who had grown up in a remote area of Arkansas. And it filled him with a sort of pride he had never experienced. He had felt it when the Alabama sailor and so many others had stood up for him that day on the shores of Guadalcanal, had expressed things like "He ain't goin' nowhere" and "He's one of us." That was the part that almost brought French to tears every time he remembered the moment.

As the days and weeks passed, French quickly became one of the most well-known African American sailors of WWII—a meteoric rise, to say the least. Radio stations and newspapers picked up his story. He was celebrated in comics, on calendars, and then came a very special collector's item: a card depicting a drawing of him pulling a raft of wounded sailors through shark-infested waters.

The card was part of a special collector's edition issued by GUM, Inc. (later called Bowman) in 1938 as war loomed on the horizon. GUM had previously produced multiple series of athletes, primarily baseball cards of popular players in the US. With war a near certainty, Warner Bowman, president of GUM, and his advertising counsel, George Moll, decided to issue a series titled "The Horrors of War," with an initial set of 240 cards. The cards would be a graphic way to showcase to the public what brutalities were occurring in the Chinese-Japanese War, the invasion of Ethiopia by Italy, and other wars—and a vehicle of promoting, hopefully, an increased desire for peace. On the back of each card was written a reference, "so people will know the horrors of war and desire peace."

National magazines and other publications brought the story of French and his heroic deeds to the attention of the public. Some articles included a picture of French in a Navy uniform, such as this one, which appeared in the newspaper publication *The Afro-American*, Baltimore, MD, November 14, 1942. Photo courtesy of Omaha World Herald.

As soon as these cards hit the market, they were extremely well-received. So sought after did they become that Bowman and Moll decided to create a set of forty-eight cards about Germany and the beginning of WWII. These were also added to as time went on.

Not long after the sinking of the *Gregory*, Charles Jackson French was featured on one of the cards, #129. It depicted the horrific night in Ironbottom Sound when he pulled fifteen sailors through the channel, saving their lives. On the back of the card was printed a brief recap of the event for which Charles was becoming famous.

GUM, Inc. card #129 celebrating the heroic deeds of Charles Jackson French in waters off Guadalcanal, September 1942, after the sinking of his ship, the USS *Gregory*. Later the picture inspired a painting created by the International Swimming Hall of Fame. Photo courtesy *Swimming World Magazine*, May 2023.

The accolades continued to come in. A serious letter-writing campaign began from different segments of the population. Many of these letters were addressed to newspapers and magazines, requesting coverage of the young hero. Understandably, French's story sparked awe and admiration from young and old alike, regardless of background, class, or education. Some of these included members from the NAACP, who wished for French to receive recognition for what he had done; others just wanted to express sincere thanks to him; still others just wished to know more about this extraordinary young man.

But numerous entreaties were mailed directly to another person with a few connections—the president of the United States of America. The letters represent the depth of response by people all across the nation to French's story of heroism.

Two of the people who wrote President Roosevelt were as different in many ways as French and his commander had been. They were Kenneth Dominique, a twelve-year-old from Texas, and Walter Weil, president of a highly respected and successful investment securities firm in New Orleans.

Kenneth's letter was handwritten and mailed on October 22, 1942, and received at the White House on October 31 while French was being honored at the football game in Omaha.

President Roosevelt
White House
Washington, D.C.

Dear President Roosevelt.

I read an article in the local newspaper concerning a brave deed by a colored man of which I am enclosing. As you see it was a great feate this article doesn't carry his name or home town. I am a school boy 12 years old in the eight grade. And colored. I would like to hear from you if possible giving me his name and home of this hero also let me know if he will be honored. I think he has done one of the bravest & grandest feate of this war so far. Thanking you for all information concerning this man also asking you to mention his name and other colored heros of this war.

I beg to remain
Yours truly

Kenneth Dominique
12 years old
704 Leal St.
San Antonio, Texas*

The letter from Mr. Walter Weil shows a remarkable interest in wanting to assure Charles Jackson French is honored in ways commensurate with his deeds. And as indicated, Mr. Weil also enclosed the newspaper article in his letter to make certain the president saw it:

Mr. Walter H. Weil, President
Weil & Company, Inc.
Investment Securities
Union Building Arcade
New Orleans, LA

The President
The White House
Washington, D.C.

Sir:

Just in case the episode described in enclosed clipping might have not come to your notice, I take great pleasure in sending it to you.

Knowing your admirable propensity to recognize heroic acts, I am sure this colored man "French" will be sought by you and when located will be commensurately commended and rewarded.

Yours very respectfully,
Walter H. Weil†

---

*   Letter from National Archives Records.
†   Letter from National Archives Records.

Among the numerous letters sent by citizens, many requests for appearances came from organizations, including veterans' groups, clubs, and also the NAACP.

In the literary world, French's deeds did not go unnoticed either. Pulitzer Prize-winning American poet William Rose Benét composed a poem in 1944 titled "The Strong Swimmer" celebrating French and his heroic deeds.[*]

I have a story fit to tell,
In head and heart a song;
A burning blue Pacific swell;
A raft that was towed along.

Out in the bloody Solomon Isles
Destroyer *Gregory* gone;
Ocean that kills for all her smiles,
And darkness coming on.

The *Gregory*'s raft bobbed on the tide
Loaded with wounded men.
Ensign and seaman clung her side.
Seaward she drifted then.

A mess-attendant, a Negro man,
Mighty of chest and limb,
Spoke up: "Til tow you all I can
As long as I can swim."

Naked, he wound his waist with a line;
Slipped smoothly overside,
Where the red bubble tells the brine
That sharks have sheared the tide.

---

[*]   Benét, William Rose, *Day of Deliverance* 1944.

"I'm going to tow this old craft in
Since we ain't got not one oar"
He breathed, as the water lapped his chin;
And he inched that raft ashore.

Strongly he stroked, and long he hauled
No breath for any song.
His wounded mates clung close, appalled.
He towed that raft along.

Clear to the eye the darkening swell
Where glimmering dangers glide;
The raft of sailors grimed from Hell
Afloat on a smoky tide.

And a dark shoulder and muscled arm
Lunging, steady and strong.
The messman, their brother, who bears a charm,
Is towing their raft along.

He gasped, "Just say if I'm go'in right!"
Yes, brother, right you are!
Danger of ocean or dark of night,
You steer by one clear star.

Six hours crawled by. . . . A barge in sight
With the raft just off the shore. . . .
The messman coughed, "Sure, I'm all right"
He was just as he was before.

And all that they knew was they called him
"French" Not quite a name to sing.
Green jungle hell or desert trench,
No man did a braver thing.

He's burned a story in my brain,
Set in my heart a song.
He and his like, by wave and main,
World without end and not in vain.

After thirty days of survivor's leave, it was time for French to return to war. But he returned widely known back home, and his fame had also spread in the Navy. His first assignment was on the USS *Endicott*.

"Well, I'm back on a destroyer—back to war," said French to himself as he walked up the ramp to board the ship. But with a new rank: he was now a Steward's Mate, 1st Class, and a famous one at that.

CHAPTER 29

Chance Discovery

". . . he was lost, and now is found." Luke 15:24

Grace Elizabeth Austin was living in Corolla, a small village on the Outer Banks in Currituck County, North Carolina, rearing their young son near her in-laws when she received a Western Union telegram from the Secretary of War: *We regret to inform you that your husband, Oswald S. Austin, is reported Missing in Action after the sinking of his ship, the USS Gregory in the waters off Guadalcanal, the Solomon Islands, 5 Sept., 1942.*

Like so many families, an MIA notification often implied the death of their loved ones, but without specific, substantiating information, it was protocol that the service member had to be reported MIA pending further clarification. In the case of a sunken ship filled with records and logs that go down with the vessel, it would usually require about a year for a notification of "presumed dead" to be sent. When Grace received her telegram, she was completely devastated.

The two had met in 1937 when Grace's aunt and uncle decided to play Cupid. Her uncle was in the Coast Guard and Oswald, who had recently joined, had been transferred to New Smyrna Beach, Florida, as a surfman, a highly specialized and dangerous assignment that mainly involved sea rescues. Oswald showed up for dinner decked out in his surfman's dress blues, very similar to a Navy chief or officer's uniform, except with a Coast Guard shield on the right sleeve and a different insignia on the hat.

After dating for about a year and a half, they were married in July 1939 and had a son the following year. The Austins named him Donald Spencer. Oswald didn't wish to use his own first name for his child—he never liked it himself.

"Call me O.S. (pronounced as two separate letters)," he would tell people, "but please, don't call me Oswald!"

During this time, Austin attended mechanic school in South Carolina which he enjoyed and displayed a natural affinity for repairing almost anything mechanical. When Pearl Harbor was bombed, he was transferred into the Navy almost immediately. His background suited him perfectly as a boatswain on the small converted destroyers which had Higgins boats that needed maintenance, and with his surfman's experience, he could maneuver in high waves to and from shore.

Grace's dear friend, "Dee," short for Dealvas Nelson, was married to a Coast Guard fellow also assigned to the Navy who had been wounded and taken to San Diego Navy Hospital. Dee decided to make the trip to see him and encouraged Grace to accompany her. The Navy had planned a mass funeral set for late October/early November in honor of the *Gregory* sailors. Grace knew it would be an emotional trip, but she decided to attend regardless. The entire family felt Oswald had perished in the sinking of the *Gregory*.

Chilly fall weather arrived early that year, but the two young women journeyed together by train from one coast to the other. It was a long, tiring trip, but Dee was determined to see her husband; Grace felt she needed some closure to the loss of her husband.

When they arrived in San Diego, Grace learned the commemorative funeral would be held in the base chapel and was scheduled shortly after they arrived. They made the decision to go to the funeral and then to the hospital. The chapel was nearly full of family members who had made the trip to attend the service, many of them softly weeping throughout the entire hour.

Afterwards, the young women left immediately for the hospital. Checking in at the front desk, Dee inquired about information as to where her husband might be located. The receptionist took a rather long time but finally said she thought he was located on the fourth floor.

"He was on third, now it appears fourth. Try fourth floor. They might have moved him, but if they did, they can tell you which floor he is located on now," the receptionist said. "We've just had so many new patients check in during the last month." She apologized for the confusion and pointed the way to the elevators.

The hospital in San Diego was indeed at capacity. The number of ships that had been shelled and the numbers of wounded Marines, Army and Air Force members had nearly overwhelmed staff throughout the facility. There were very few private rooms. Most floors consisted of huge bays and walls were lined on both sides with beds; overflow was located out in the hallways. Doctors, nurses, patients, and visitors were bustling everywhere.

When they entered the crowded elevator, Dee looked at Grace. "Now, what floor did that lady say? Was it third or fourth?"

When the doors opened on the third floor, people were getting off, and both young women were pushed forward.

Dee shrugged. "Guess we'll try this," she said.

They turned toward the right where they could see through double doors into a large bay filled with patients in beds. As they rounded the corner, there was a bed right next to the door. Grace stopped in her tracks. She threw her hand up to her mouth to stifle a cry and grabbed Dee by the arm. "Look!"

Grace pointed at the man in the bed. He had several tubes running from various places on his body, and his eyes were closed. With two quick steps she was at his side and bent over his face, with her hands lightly on his arm.

"Oswald, dear," she half-cried, half-whispered. "Dearest, it's me, Grace."

With obvious effort, Oswald slowly opened his eyes and stared at her. He squinted, trying to make sense of it all. Slowly, it looked as if a light was turning on and his lips parted slightly.

"Gracie?" he said, in a hoarse, halting whisper. "Is that you?"

During the next forty-eight hours, Oswald Austin's memory, though still foggy, began to return. While Grace remained by his side, struggling to keep from crying one moment and laughing the next, her friend Dee hastened off to find a doctor or charge nurse, anyone who could help them get things straightened out.

Quickly, a nurse with a hospital staff member from Records came to begin obtaining all the information necessary for processing paperwork for Oswald Spencer Austin, Navy coxswain, former Coast Guard surfman, and a survivor of the sinking of the USS *Gregory*, September 5, 1942.

Oswald was alive, but he was in terrible shape, both mentally and physically. Finally, a physician came to speak to Grace and her husband to update them both.

"We've been wondering who this was," he began. "And quite frankly, we were hesitant to treat him too aggressively, since we've not been able to make much out of what he can say—mostly disjointed statements—he's not been able to communicate to us who he was or what happened to him. We even had a representative from military records come by and wanted to write him up for not being in uniform when he arrived! It's been chaotic."

Grace could only shake her head in disbelief. The joy of finding Oswald alive was quickly replaced with a new reality—the pitiable condition of her husband both physically and mentally. Since being admitted, he had not been able to communicate in any appreciable way but exhibited extreme discomfort, seemingly from abdominal pain. However, the only outward evidence of injuries was on his legs, especially his knees. They assumed he probably had been through some sort of explosion, given that O.S. couldn't articulate anything coherent since he had arrived at the hospital in San Diego. All the attending medical staff could do was done based on conjecture.

However, once Oswald saw his wife, Grace, his mind began to clear rather quickly. And the harrowing events surrounding the night when he was standing on the bridge of the *Gregory* with his Skipper, Lieutenant Commander Bauer, and they suddenly took a direct hit out of the black night began flooding back into his consciousness.

"Did he live?" he suddenly asked Grace. "Cap'n Bauer. Did he make it?"

"I don't know, honey," she said quietly to him. "I believe he's still on the missing in action list."

Oswald turned his face toward the wall and began crying softly, with sounds more like whimpering noises. Grace bent over and laid her head gently on his shoulder. Oswald took her hand and squeezed it as hard as he could.*

---

* Interviews with Don Austin, son of Oswald Austin.

CHAPTER 30

Back to War

"He leads me beside still waters; He restores my soul . . . "
Psalm 23:2–3

After an avalanche of deserved attention for Charles's heroic swim, the time came to report back to the Navy. He had spent his thirty days survivor's leave with Viola, his sister, in Omaha. She was so proud of her brother—all his siblings were—for saving so many lives on Guadalcanal. But Viola hated to see him return, knowing war was still raging in the Pacific and all things pointed to a second front opening up any day in the Atlantic. She worried about him. He drank more than he should—he said it was to calm his nerves but she could hear him crying out at night in his sleep. Sometimes he became so agitated, she would go into his room to check on him. Most of the time Viola found him completely drenched in sweat.

Ironically, when his new orders reached him, it was on December 7, 1942, the one-year anniversary of the bombing of Pearl Harbor. He was to report for duty on a newly commissioned destroyer, the USS *Endicott*, in Bremerton, Washington, with a promotion to Steward's Mate First Class.

The widespread publicity that Charles had received did not go unnoticed by the Navy. On December 2, 1942, Admiral Kelly Turner, Commander of the Amphibious Forces, Pacific, wrote a letter of recommendation for Charles to receive the Silver Star Medal for his gallant deeds in Ironbottom Sound on September 4 and 5 following the sinking of the *Gregory*. Nothing, however, materialized from Admiral Turner's recommendation.

Charles continued to struggle with balancing the tragic and disastrous results of the surface battles in the Solomons with his return to daily responsibilities. Having shore leave, where alcohol was easily available, only seemed to be a temptation that resulted in too much revelry. On March 2, 1943, he was arrested by Shore Patrol for refusing to show his ID card. To add to the confusion, he refused to give his ship's name and was charged with being out after his liberty had ended. Not long after this incident, Charles was back in the hospital for treatment due to alcohol-related issues.

But this particular hospitalization in early 1943 resulted in a completely new direction for his life—and a much-welcomed one. He met a lovely young woman whose name was Jettie Mae Benton. She was working as a nursing attendant and happened to be the sister of someone Charles already knew—Stacy A. Benton, a chief steward in the Navy. Charles wasted no time learning as much as he could about her. She had been in the San Diego Naval Hospital since the beginning of the war, but the two hadn't crossed paths until now. Charles and Jettie Mae would marry in September of 1944.

Knowing time was short before French would be leaving again, they saw each other as much as possible. However, by the beginning of April 1943 Charles Jackson French was headed back to war—this time, to the Atlantic on the *Endicott* to escort two convoys of troops to Africa and then to Ireland. These were vital missions ahead of the future invasion of Europe but saturated with potential dangers from German U-boats and enemy aircraft. The German subs patrolled in large groups dubbed "Wolf Packs," for their ferocious stalking of troop ships. Charles had exchanged one body of dangerous water for another.

The hellish depths of the Atlantic were a match for the terrifying waters of Ironbottom Sound, especially in the area known as the Pit, that 300-mile gap in the mid-Atlantic with no air cover. It represented a sort of "No Man's Land"—or in this case, "No Man's Water."

The U-boats were relentless, and many times Charles heard the now all too familiar blare of "*General Quarters, General Quarters, all hands man your battle stations!*"

By the time the *Endicott* returned to the States, Charles required another few days in the hospital due to mental health concerns, this time in New York. One of the first things he did was to call Jettie Mae, who made the long cross-country trip to see him at the Naval Hospital in Brooklyn. Besides being reunited with Jettie Mae, Charles learned that his rating had been changed to Steward's Mate 1st Class and he had been given temporary duty assignment back in San Diego to attend Cooks and Stewards school, which he did, finally graduating with the highest possible grade: 4.0. For a while, things seemed to be coming together for him.

Yet, the aftereffects of the experience in Ironbottom Sound lingered. And there wasn't a day he didn't think about all the men lost the night the *Gregory* and *Little* went down . . . most especially, the Skipper.

CHAPTER 31

Commemoration

"Father of the fatherless and protector of widows is God in His holy habitation." Psalm 68:5

The letter that Jackie Bauer dreaded receiving, yet the one she was grateful to receive, arrived on September 6, 1943, a year and a day after the sinking of the *Gregory*. It was the official notification from the Department of Navy Personnel that her husband, after the passing of a year, was presumed dead. Harry F. Bauer could now be officially mourned, honored, released. Closure. It was a bittersweet day for Jackie. Her daughter, Mimi, who had always been the apple of her daddy's eye, was now eight years old. Though she was more aware of what was transpiring at this point in time, she really only carried a few distant memories of her dad.

Lieutenant Commander Bauer was promoted to Commander, posthumously. In the following months, both Harry Bauer and Gus Lofberg, who perished during the ferocious surface engagement in the early morning hours of September 5, 1942, were honored by having ships named after them. The USS *Harry F. Bauer* was launched as destroyer DD-738 at the Bath Iron Works in Bath, Maine. Gladys "Jackie" Boyd Bauer, who sponsored the ship, attended the launching ceremony on July 9, 1944, with her nine-year-old daughter, Mimi. The destroyer had been converted to a minelayer and commissioned for duty in September, two years following the death of Jackie Bauer's husband.

About the same time, the USS *Lofberg*, named for Commander Gus B. Lofberg, was laid down on November 4, 1943, by Bethlehem Steel Co. in San Francisco and launched on August 12, 1944. The ship was sponsored by Gus's widow, Norma Costella of Santa Cruz, and both she and their daughter, Lynn, attended the ceremony. In later years, the USS *Lofberg* saw action in both the Korean War and Far Eastern tours of duty during the 1960s.

The two friends, Harry Bauer and Gus Lofberg, who had shared so many experiences together during their lives, now shared one more significant event—having ships named in their honor, posthumously.

CHAPTER 32

The War That Lingers

". . . no refuge remains to me; no one cares for my soul."
Psalm 142:4

Unlike French or Adrian, who were released after their treatment from the Naval Hospital, San Diego, for thirty days survivor's leave, Oswald Austin faced a longer road of rehabilitation. Once Grace discovered him by chance in the hospital, his memory returned, at least for the most part. But talking to him for only a few minutes revealed remaining issues. His mind seemed to wander, and his responses to statements or questions often made no sense at all. So the decision by the medical team in San Diego was that he needed additional treatment. As a result, he was sent to a psychiatric health facility in Texas for continued rest and evaluation. Later, the war veteran was processed and finally released on disability in New Orleans.

After Austin retired from the Navy due to health reasons, he continued to be plagued with severe abdominal issues. He returned home to Grace and his young son, Don, who was now nearly four years old. They had been living with Oswald's parents while he was away during the war.

Oswald's homecoming received mixed reviews. Instead of greeting him with open arms, his little boy ran and hid. "Who is this man—I don't know him," said the youngster, eyeing this person who was a complete stranger to him. Oswald had envisioned a different welcome and immediately erupted into anger and derision: "Why, he's nothing but a mama's boy!"

In the following weeks, townspeople, especially those who knew Grace and the Austin family, were more than willing to give Oswald a job. But something always seemed to arise; Austin's response to any small problem or issue was disruptive and usually escalated quickly. It was several years before he could hold down a steady job for any length of time.

Even as a boy growing up, Oswald had loved to ride horses. And for most of his life, he had owned one, especially during his teen years, when he rounded up a herd of cattle along the Outer Banks. After he returned home from the war, one of the first things he did was to acquire a horse once again.

Oswald had heard about an injured Arabian with a broken leg through a neighbor. The horse was going to be put down, but Oswald talked the owner into giving him the horse to see what he could do about the leg.

On his property was an empty wooden shed about the size of a garage with openings at both ends. Oswald rigged a system of ropes that allowed the horse to stand but kept weight off the broken limb. Slowly, with constant care, O.S. was able to nurse the horse back to health, even to the point that the Arabian could take a rider. Oswald always walked the horse gently and never rode him hard so as not to overdo the weakened leg. The horse was, without question, therapy for the veteran.

However, one evening the Austin family was listening to a radio show featuring a skit about soldiers in the war. It was promoted as a slapstick comedy, a silly reenactment of life in the army, and made comic references to the horrendous wartime events or devastating consequences.

Oswald listened for a while, until his anger turned to seething indignation. He sprang from his chair and stormed out of the house and saddled his horse. He was gone all night, and Grace had no idea where he was or if he was safe. Finally, the following morning Oswald retuned home, both rider and horse seemingly none the worse for wear. But this became a pattern: any type of violent program or something adverse pertaining to the war would ruin his mental state. A small matter could quickly produce an angry and escalated response.

It wasn't until the early 1960s that Austin met a doctor who became sincerely interested in his case and listened intently to the veteran's list of physical complaints, especially pertaining to his abdominal issues. Instead of attributing these "supposed" maladies to his severe emotional challenges, this doctor suggested exploratory surgery. Oswald, though skeptical, consented.

The day of the operation arrived, and when the team of surgeons cut into the abdominal cavity, they couldn't believe what they saw. The twenty-to-thirty-foot plummet from the bridge to the deck below the night the *Gregory* was shelled had severely damaged nearly all of his internal organs—rupturing blood vessels, tearing tissue, severing ligaments. In addition, some lower ribs were shattered. As time went by, without any surgical intervention, some of the bruised and torn organ tissue had grown back and were connected by scar tissue that fused them together—one organ abnormally conjoined to another—nature's attempt to heal. In a few places, tissue was connected to the wall of the stomach and lower lungs.

During the next few hours, the surgeons snipped and clipped to release pressure and restore more accurate anatomical positioning of organs and normal functions. After Oswald healed from the reconstructive surgery, he told his family he had lost all hope of living without pain until this operation. Though there continued to be many struggles, O.S.'s emotional health steadily improved. Before long, he was able to work and return to a more stable lifestyle. Outbursts, however, could be easily triggered from seemingly harmless events.

In the years following the war, the lieutenant who had served with him on the *Gregory* as officer of the landing craft contacted him several times. In fact, Lieutenant Heinrich Heine had even visited his wounded shipmate several times while he was still in the hospital. The two men had conducted several nerve-racking missions together in the deadly waters of Guadalcanal.

Heine was the young officer in charge of the landing boat with Oswald as coxswain when they were delivering supplies to the Raiders on Guadalcanal—and ran aground. The two of them were then involved in a skirmish with the Raiders who captured a Japanese soldier. It was that event which led to O.S. possessing three Japanese coins—the only thing found in his possession after he was rescued following the sinking of the *Gregory*. The good-natured and caring former Navy lieutenant made several attempts to get O.S. to come with him to reunions or meetings of APD crews and veterans, but to no avail. Oswald enjoyed visiting with Heine but always said he didn't wish to go to any group get-togethers. "No," O.S. would always say, shaking his head, "I wouldn't care to do that."

One thing, however, remained with him until the day he died. Though positive proof remained elusive, in the back of Oswald Austin's mind, he had always suspected that the commanding officer of the *Gregory*, Lieutenant Commander Harry Bauer, had forfeited his own life in order to save him.

Oswald knew he had been standing right next to the Skipper when the bridge had been shelled and exploded. In fact, he was in the process of telling Bauer about the adventure he and Lt. Heine had encountered with the Raiders on the beach. Both Austin and Bauer had been blown to the deck below, landing not far apart. Oswald, in total agony, began screaming for help, unable to move any part of his body. And he vaguely remembered two shipmates pulling him into the water and then heaving him onto a raft between two other sailors. After that, all Oswald could recall was looking up at the black sky, then the sensation that he was lying in a large puddle of something very warm.

For the remainder of Oswald Austin's life, one solitary thought haunted him and seemed to return again and again: Did Harry Bauer place his, Oswald's, life above his own? And if so, the question lingered: *What is the sum total of debt owed to someone who sacrifices, willingly, their life to save yours?*

Oswald Spencer Austin, US Coast Guard (ret.), participant of the WWII Invasion of the Solomon Islands, participant in vital missions transporting and supplying Marine Raiders, and survivor of the sinking of the USS *Gregory* (APD-3), died on March 1, 2002.

CHAPTER 33

Beyond Ironbottom Sound

". . . Even though I walk through the valley of the shadow of death, I will fear no evil . . . for You are with me . . ." Psalm 23:4

Charles Jackson French and his wife, Jettie Mae, continued to reside in San Diego after Charles retired from the service. Like so many others who had been through the traumatizing events of war, he continued to search for peace. Some days were more difficult than others.

The nation continued to hunger for war news, especially after the invasion of Europe took place on June 6, 1944. Those combined forces of Allied planes, ships, and armies comprised the largest amphibious invasion in all of military history. As the country turned its attention toward Europe, previous events, especially the first initial engagements in the South Pacific, began to dim. It wasn't a matter of people not caring or becoming disinterested; it was that the war had increased exponentially with the opening of a second front that encompassed most of Europe.

As the years progressed, it appears Charles continued to suffer with what most likely was PTSD (post-traumatic stress disorder), as it is referred to today. He often thought about the things that happened in the Pacific, but nothing touched his emotions more than remembering that day on the beaches of Guadalcanal when several white sailors and Raiders had declared so forcefully, "He's staying here—French belongs with us." The memory of that absolute display of acceptance by the other sailors and Marines stayed with him for the remainder of his life.

Charles Jackson French died only one decade later, after the end of WWII, on November 7, 1956, two weeks after his thirty-seventh birthday. He was buried at Fort Rosecrans National Cemetery, a federal military cemetery on the tip of Point Loma in San Diego. His passing was hardly noticed, except by family. Unlike the weeks immediately following his heroic deeds in Guadalcanal, his death rated only a paragraph or two in a local newspaper.

Jettie Mae remained in San Diego working at the Naval Hospital where the couple had first met, rearing their daughter who had been born in the late 1940s. She was active in her church, Logan Temple A.M.E. Zion Church, where she was president of the Altar Guild. In addition, she was president of the Auxiliary of the Jesse Thomas Post, Veterans of Foreign Wars.

On November 17, 1968, Jettie Mae French, age fifty-one, suffered a fatal heart attack in her home. She was also buried in Fort Rosecrans National Cemetery next to her husband, Charles Jackson French, a little-known WWII hero.

CHAPTER 34

Remembering, 1993

". . . each one's work will become manifest, for the Day will disclose it, because it will be revealed by fire, and the fire will test what sort of work each one has done." 1 Corinthians 3:13

The Adrians quietly left the funeral service for one of Bob's classmates at the Academy, the Class of 1943. Commonly referred to as "the 43ers," his class held two singular distinctions in the annals of Naval Academy history: they were the only class to be graduated in an accelerated three-year program due to the beginning of World War II, and they had the largest number of lost and never returned. Both these distinctions remain true today.

After the couple had embraced those in attendance at the service—all of them lifelong friends—they decided to walk past the memorial honoring those in his class who had fallen and were never found. Then, Bob would walk around to the monument with the names engraved under the Class of 1927 and find once again, as he had done countless times over the past fifty-plus years, the names of Harry Bauer and Gus Lofberg, commanders of the *Gregory* and *Little* respectively.

On the way home, Bob asked Joan to drop him off at the bench. Of course she knew where he meant. By tradition, each Naval Academy class contributes something as a remembrance—a beautiful stained-glass window, a piece of statuary, or other artwork—to commemorate their time at the Yard. The Class of 1943 had dedicated a bench called the Compass Rose bench located near the Spa Creek Sea Wall. As time had passed, this place had become one of Bob's favorite spots to sit, enjoy the views of the water, and get lost in his memories.

He was particularly pensive on this day. "We are dwindling," he thought, remembering so many he had served with who had died before they could return home. And of those that were fortunate enough to come back alive, many had passed away in the meantime. The remaining 43ers were very close, keeping in touch with one another frequently.

Bob sat on the bench reflecting on his own Navy career that had spanned nearly twenty-seven years, including several WWII events, a major part of his history. As soon as he had recovered from the wounds acquired the night the *Gregory* went down, he had resumed active duty—and returned to the war in the Pacific.

The second ship he was assigned to was the USS *Boyd*. There, his commanding officer was Ulysses S. Grant Sharp Jr., nicknamed "Oley"; the later four-star admiral was named for his relative, General Grant, who had married Oley's great-aunt. Adrian took to him immediately and soon found himself back in the thick of things. But what Bob truly delighted in was that Oley had been a 1927 classmate of Harry Bauer— had been a close friend of this commander Adrian had so respected.

However, smooth sailing wasn't to be found on the *Boyd* either. During exercises in the South Pacific near the island of Nauru, which was not believed to hold Japanese troops, the Boyd came under direct fire from shore. One of the first salvo of rounds struck the ship below the waterline. It entered the forward Fire Room and detonated on the bulkhead of the forward Engine Room, rupturing the main steam lines in the areas. Instantly, seventeen sailors plus the chief engineer were burned to death.

Bob was in charge of the detail for recovering the bodies and preparing them for burial at sea the following day. Their remains were wrapped in canvas and weighted with a five-inch shell to ensure they would sink to the bottom. "It was a grim occasion for all of us," thought Bob, "that day on the *Boyd*, December 3, 1943. Two days of infamy for me— September 5, 1942 and December 3, 1943—about a year apart."

In his total career, he had served or commanded seven ships, and afterwards helped set up the Navy's ROTC unit at Auburn University. Later, he became the secretary-treasurer of the Naval Institute Press.

But regardless of how many interesting assignments or challenging duties he had had in the Navy, it was really impossible to forget all the events during that very first duty assignment as an ensign: the very first day when he swung over on a boatswain's chair. The Raiders had looked down at this freshly caught fish and booed his embarking the *Gregory*, especially since he was loaded down with a huge box of gear, which included his beautiful Naval Academy sword and scabbard. All these belongings went down with the ship, settling somewhere in the depths of Ironbottom Sound.

He laughed out loud at the thought of that embarkation. About ten years after the war, his wife, Joan, had surprised him with a new sword which adorned a special place in his home wardroom. His thoughts then turned to his initial meeting with the Skipper, then later French, O.S.— everyone. "Wonder if they are all still alive—and if so, what they are doing now?" he asked himself.

When the war was over, Bob had done his best to touch base with as many who returned home as he could. He made a special effort to reach out to families who had lost loved ones with whom he had served. He sent Academy announcements to Harry Bauer's wife to keep her informed of events there. Then later, after Jackie Bauer's death, he continued to send clippings and Navy articles to Mimi, the Bauers' daughter.

But try as he might, by the time he returned from the war and began new duties, there was scant information he could find on the messmate he knew as French. He had done the NBC broadcast to commemorate French in 1942, shortly after they had returned home, but in later years, was unable to find out where he was and what he was doing.

"They were incredible men," he thought, "both of them." Bob lowered his head for a moment and took a deep breath. *"All* of them," he whispered. Bob Adrian stood up, looking out across the waters for a moment, then turned toward home.

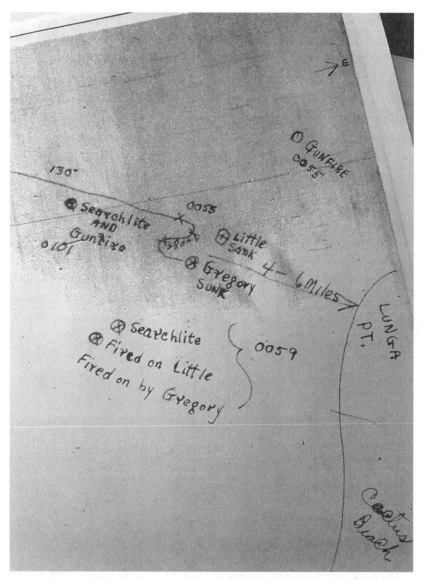

Bob Adrian's personal sketch of the positions of the *Gregory* and the *Little* on the night of September 4–5, when both ships were attacked by Japanese destroyers. Photo courtesy of the Adrian Family collection.

In later life, Bob Adrian also experienced the lingering effects of war. Several years later, he had intermittent difficulty with nightmares disturbing his sleep. He began to retreat into his own world with too much alcohol. His wife and family recognized what was happening and entreated him to quit—which he did. He redoubled his efforts to keep in touch with and support those he knew who had been in the war as well as their families.

Robert Nelson Adrian, Captain USN, died March 1, 2011, at the Arleigh Burke Nursing Facility, where he resided in the last couple of years of his life and continued to journal about his Navy experiences. His family said that just shortly before his death, there had been a routine testing of the fire alarm equipment. Though the veteran was medicated and resting, he immediately awakened, shouting as loud as he could and trying to get out of bed: "Let's go! Let's go! We need to get the boys out!"

Some memories live forever. And though many who were there in Ironbottom Sound never made it home, may their memories live on.

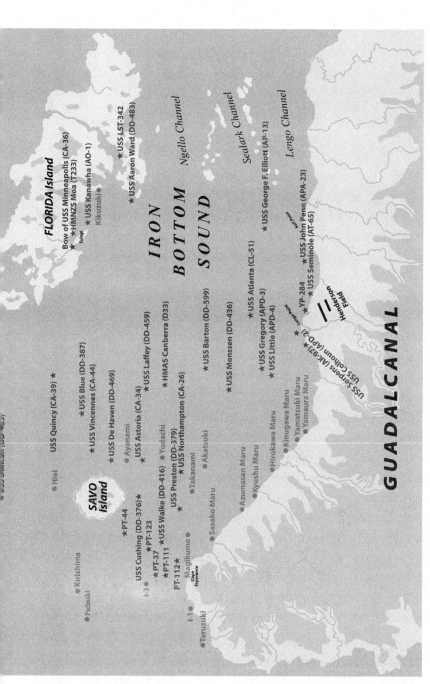

Overall map of ships that sank in Sealark Channel during WWII; the channel was renamed Ironbottom Sound. Japanese ships are designated with a circle; US and allied ships with a star. Most of these ships were lost during Fall 1942. Courtesy of Navy Military Archives.

Epilogue

May 8, 1945, marked V-E Day: Victory in Europe. German Marshall Wilheim Keitel, along with two other high-ranking German leaders, signed surrender documents in Karlshorst, Berlin, making it official.

Four months later, on the other side of the world, on September 2, 1945, formal surrender documents were signed by Japanese envoys Foreign Minister Mamoru Shigemitsu and General Yoshijiro Umezu aboard the USS *Missouri*.

The war was over.

At least, formally.

For the better part of five years, nearly every country across the globe had participated, in some capacity and to some extent, in the great conflict. The number of estimated deaths worldwide is staggering: battle deaths are often recorded as 15 million; battle wounded as 25 million; civilian deaths set at 45 million. And with warfare so widespread, it's understandable that global casualty estimates—both military and civilian—would vary significantly in multiple sources. For example, as reported by the National WWII Museum in New Orleans, "The number of civilian deaths in China alone might well be more than 50,000,000."[*]

Little wonder then, when official news of the end of the war came, jubilation spread across every village, town, city, and nation. People were

---

[*] "Research Starters: Worldwide Deaths in World War II" at nationalww2museum .org; also see Appendix D: Worldwide Deaths in WWII by Country.

just eager to get back to normal—living their lives, raising their families, having their loved ones with them again.

Yet it would be impossible for the consequences of such great turmoil and warfare to slip quietly into the night. And even more impossible to ever hear all the deeds, whether heroic and sacrificial or heartbreaking and terrifying—much less to record them: each and every soul that participated in any sort of capacity in WWII came home with a story.

Nonetheless, these experiences would take an incalculable toll. Most of the men who returned from the war were wounded to some extent or another and would experience lingering effects. Most of the men who survived the sinking of the *Gregory* experienced these aftereffects. Certainly French and Austin did, as well as many others.

As the months and years passed, however, many of these returning warriors were forgotten and their deeds faded. It wasn't because people were not thankful for the sacrifices or commitment or bravery. It was just that living their own lives required attention. Within a mere four years after World War II, the Korean War appeared on the horizon. War once more invaded the minds and thoughts of daily life in America.

Fortunately, during the last few years, attention is being given to some of the lesser-known heroes from WWII. Two years ago, the training pool at San Diego Naval Base was renamed for Charles Jackson French.

And just a few months ago, Secretary of the Navy Carlos del Toro announced a new Arleigh Burke-class destroyer will be named for French—a beautiful and welcomed tribute for a true American hero.

The USS *Gregory* was indeed a microcosm of our nation in this sense: her crew hailed from all over America, from widely varying backgrounds and levels of education, different life experiences, dispositions, and personalities.

Still, for all their differences, they bonded together for a common mission and a shared desire to complete it. They worked together to accomplish that goal . . . and to survive.

Banners featuring Charles Jackson French at the San Diego Naval Base training pool. Photo courtesy of the Naval Base San Diego.

And regardless of their differences, there was a far greater commonality. Wherever valor, courage, or bravery surfaced, it was drawn from deep within—far beyond any of the dissimilarities of each individual service member: to the point that the contrasts themselves became superficial.

When faced with the ultimate outcome of death for friends and fellow warriors, valor more often than not showed up . . . in all its glory.

Acknowledgments

During research for my book, *Marine Raiders: The True Story of the Legendary WWII Battalions*, I continued to run across mention of the "brave little ships" designated APDs ("AP" for Transport, literally Auxiliary Personnel, and "D" for Destroyer) used to transport Raiders. Maybe my interest in them was fueled by the fact that they were almost always brushed over; their missions, though vital, seldom heralded; and their engagements, though brutal, usually referred to as minor. The ships had minimal armament with which to defend themselves and were relatively slow besides. Perhaps they just seemed like the proverbial underdogs.

But contrary to the APDs' lack of notoriety, the WWII Marine Raiders who depended on these transports to get them to their targets often referred to these ships with great admiration. In fact, these hard-nosed Raiders who walked with swagger actually "loved" the crews of these ships—that's the word the Raiders most frequently used when referring to the APDs and everyone on them.

As I researched and scoured through documents, I found some stories involving the USS *Gregory*, APD-3, that were particularly amazing—truly compelling, gripping, heroic stories. As far as I could tell, many of these events involving the *Gregory* and her sister ship, the *Little*, had been almost completely overlooked. So, after *Marine Raiders* was completed, I decided to dig further. And as the saying goes, the rest is history—in this case, literally. These are some of the most intriguing military history stories I've ever encountered.

I began the sometimes frustrating process of locating relatives of men who had been on the *Gregory* that I wished to write about. It wasn't easy. But once we connected, I found all of them were as excited to tell me their relatives' stories as I was about writing them.

So of the many to whom I owe thanks and gratitude, I must begin with the families who helped me piece together this story. They all have been so gracious to me by putting up with my frequent phone calls, emails, and endless questions. This book really belongs to you and your heroic WWII relatives—your dads, grandfathers, uncles, and cousins.

I'll begin first with the Robert Nelson Adrian family. Through his daughter, Judy Adrian Deckers, I learned so much about Bob Adrian. After the sinking of the *Gregory*, he went on to enjoy a twenty-five-year career that was extremely rewarding for him and his family. Judy sent numerous stories to me as well as sharing pages from her dad's journals, photos, and newspaper clippings. Bob Adrian's eyewitness accounts breathe life into this story. I wish I could have visited with him in his basement Wardroom and listened to the stories firsthand. But Bob Adrian, who was pure Navy, comes alive through his children and his journals. Sincere thanks to all the Adrian family for sharing with me.

My sincere thanks to Linda and Chester French. Mr. French is the nephew of Charles Jackson French, one of the primary heroes of this story. Charles's deeds during WWII in the dangerous waters of Guadalcanal are truly unbelievable. For many years they have gone unrecognized, but recently the Secretary of the Navy, the Honorable Carlos del Toro, has helped to adjust that oversight by naming a ship after this WWII hero. Thank you so much, Linda and Chester, for talking to me and sending along some great information.

To Bryan Condra, who is the great-nephew of Commander Harry F. Bauer, I give great appreciation for sharing many family treasures. Bryan sent numerous pictures from family albums, many of which we have reproduced in the book. He also possesses the original wheeled field spurs that Harry Bauer as a boy loved to see on his father's knee-high calvary boots. The Bauer-Condra family tree is filled with military members who have served over the decades in many different wars, in many different places, and in many different capacities.

The same is true for the family of Oswald Spencer Austin, who was in the Coast Guard, then was transitioned into the Navy after the bombing of Pearl Harbor. His son, Don Austin, was so patient and gracious to take my many calls to check on stories, dates, and details. And in the Austin family, Don himself retired from the Navy after twenty-two years, a Senior Chief Aviation Electrician's Mate, and recently attended his son's retirement ceremony—Spencer Pell Austin, Captain, USN. The Austins represent five successive generations of career military service in the Coast Guard and US Navy.

My sincere gratitude to all these people who tirelessly took my phone calls and answered my questions. I'm truly humbled and honored to be able to record and share with others these stories, and I know readers will love reading about the fine, patriotic men and the families that supported them.

It's always great to get input from people who have personal knowledge of your subject matter. Captain Paul Hauser (Ret.) spent many hours reading the manuscript to make certain terminology, customs, and sequences were correct. No amount of research can replace the knowledge of someone who has "been there/done that." It was fascinating and enlightening to hear terms that are actually used on ships. Paul, thank you so much for your time and excellent attention to detail!

Another person with personal experience is present-day Marine Raider John A. Daily who was a team leader in the vital and esteemed Detachment One after 9/11. John read chapters and gave me firsthand information on many scenarios, such as what it's really like to scramble down cargo nets loaded with gear and into craft below bouncing violently in high seas. Many thanks, John, for your encouragement along the way. Looking forward to reading your own autobiography, *Tough Rugged Bastards*.

Also, heartfelt thanks to my personal friends, Kathy and Dave Brock, for their information also drawn from personal experience. Dave is a twenty-three-year Navy veteran who retired as an AOCM (Master Chief Aviation Ordanceman) who served primarily on carriers and gave me valuable insight into daily happenings on a large ship. And I learned what "mid-rats" stands for—midnight rations! Kathy is also a Navy veteran who worked in records. As such she was invaluable in taking official WWII Navy records that I had received and helping me understand what I was looking at. She even created a timetable of Charles Jackson French's service for determining where he had served during his two enlistments. Added to that, her own father had been a mess attendant in WWII. Thank you both so much for your encouragement, information, insight, and most of all, your friendship.

Now to some people who have been indispensable over the past decade as I've pursued my passion of recording as many of these WWII stories as possible: Sincere thanks to my agent, Greg Johnson, president of Wordserve Literary and FaithHappenings.com for appreciating a good war story and then finding the right publisher for all these projects. Thank you, Greg—it all begins with you.

Next, my gracious Lord has provided me with a wonderful trio of brilliant people that I affectionately call "My Team."

First, to Brenda Holder, my "personal editor," for reading behind me on each chapter (sometimes rereading maybe more than once and, in this case, more than twice) and providing vital input. Often, she can nail a thought or word I had been searching for—and couldn't come up with—in remarkable ways. On this particular book, she has truly been a warrior herself as we pursued information and correct terminology on a host of items. In addition, Bren, I count on your encouragement! You are a true friend and more importantly . . . a prayer partner.

Along these lines, many thanks to Jim Wortham for scanning and helping with photos—your work is always wonderful; and to artist Bret Melvin, whose illustrations add such great dimension and visual information to the text. These two are also prayer warriors I can count on. Hopefully, we will have many more projects together.

And of course, my love and thanks to my dear husband who reads first drafts, offers suggestions and encouragement, especially during crunch time when he listens patiently to my frustrations and complaints, then rejoices with me in the victories. There would be no books without you, sweetheart! Thanks for your forbearance and kindness as I push forward pursuing my dream of recording the biographies of men and women in our country's service—deeds we need to remember.

Next, as a believer in the Lord Jesus Christ, I want to thank God for leading me to this amazing story and to all these wonderful people who have helped me. We are so blessed to live in a country where we are free—and that freedom is due to the unbelievable sacrifices of our men and women in our military—all branches, all jobs, all contributions. It always sounds a bit cliche but is certainly not meant to be—our sincere thanks to all of you.

And now one last thing. It took many years of difficult living before realizing something was missing in my life. After reaching the end of my rope, so to speak, I found the Lord Jesus Christ—or to say it more accurately, He found me. If you feel you are missing something in your life, I urge you to consider placing it in His competent hands. He gave His life so that we might live: He takes us out of troubled waters . . . and places us on a safe shore to live with Him forever.

Family Tributes

Heroes

A Tribute to our parents: Robert Nelson Adrian and Joan Smith Adrian.

They were Americans born in the second decade of the new twentieth century. They were descendants of emigrants who had ventured across their new nation, traveling by wagon on the Oregon Trail, seeking freedom and a better way of life. In that day, the word "hero" was held to a very high standard—tremendous sacrifice and hardship were the norm. It is not surprising that when the next generation was called to defend their country from the grave threat of WWII, they signed up without hesitation, united in courage and patriotism.

They did not call themselves "heroes" but, in retrospect and humble appreciation, they have become known as part of the Greatest Generation. Growing up, our father seldom spoke of the war except to tell the story of one man he called a hero: African American mess attendant Charles Jackson French. As voiced in our father's words on a 1942 NBC broadcast and recorded in a lifetime of letters written up to his final days in recognition of French, he felt it an injustice that our country had not bestowed on this man the military's highest medal for heroism, the Medal of Honor. Every descendant of the fifteen servicemen he saved that night owed Charles Jackson their life. He literally pulled our injured, oil-covered fathers from the water and swam, towing the raft all night in shark-infested waters. It is a testament of character that those fifteen men, upon rescue, would not allow this man to be segregated from them due to his skin color. He was a hero.

Our father lived his life by example, and it was one of honor, integrity, loyalty, and service. He was a gentle, kind man. The strongest language from him would be an occasional "damn!" The expletive usually involved a loss by either the Navy football team or his Baltimore Orioles. Following retirements from his beloved Navy, then banking and his many civic volunteer jobs, he finally had time. He loved filling it with grandchildren, trips to the family beach house and biking the circumference of the Naval Academy. But he increasingly felt the urgency to write his stories.

Many of us wondered why he chose to set up a home office in the basement of our 100-year-old Annapolis house located just outside of the Academy's walls instead of in one of the sunlit rooms upstairs. However, it was soon apparent it was because he felt comfortable, as if aboard ship. The basement was not only dark, but it moaned and groaned with the old pipes and enormous black furnace that shared his space. At his desk he could keep track of the comings and goings of the family by the sound of footsteps on hardwood floors above.

Here he surrounded himself with pictures of all his ships, the Admirals he had served, and beloved shipmates. The small bathroom even had a handwritten sign, "The Head." He smoked his pipe. He loved it. Here he wrote and wrote, completing a voluminous journal over the years called "Life of a Sailor and his Family." He wrote it for his four children, eight grandchildren, and many great-grandchildren. Now we feel the importance of these stories for all future generations. We treasure and pass them on with tremendous love, admiration, and gratitude for our father, our mother, and for all those of that Greatest Generation. Our heroes.

Judy Adrian Decker, Robert Nelson Adrian Jr., James Leahy Adrian, and Joan Adrian Krafft, sons and daughters of Robert Nelson Adrian, Captain, US Navy, WWII

Postscript by Judy Adrian Decker

I must admit, I've felt somewhat guilty in writing this tribute to my dad; I feel this only because our mother deserves her own book. She is a legend to almost all that knew her. It is a testament to our dad how strongly we felt his love and strength. This was a man who spent most of his life at sea. Our shore duty tours were the best of times, but when Dad was at sea, we were Navy strong. Today I think always of our mother's positive, joyful strength. What a celebration it was when Dad's ship came in. I have heard every compliment of our beautiful mother, but the one I love the most is: "She was the tent pole."

Tribute to Charles Jackson French

"Our family would like for people to see the value of sacrifice and to understand that French's story is an American story." Roscoe Harris, nephew of Charles Jackson French, *Omaha Forum*.

"It's nice to see him finally get the recognition he deserves. The key thing is, it's a story that should be known across the country. He was a hero and people don't know it." Chester French, nephew of Charles Jackson French, *San Diego Union-Tribune*.

Tribute to Merritt A. Edson

My grandfather, the late Major General Merritt A. Edson, USMC, was an early advocate of the APDs and their use in reconnaissance, raids, and other special operations. Then as commanding officer of the First Marine Raiders during the Tulagi and Guadalcanal campaigns, the APDs were an invaluable asset in the Raiders being able to carry out their mission successfully. The dedication and sacrifice made by the officers and crews of the APDs were an indispensable part in winning the Guadalcanal campaign and the war. Having read and enjoyed immensely *Marine Raiders: The True Story of the Legendary WWII Battalions* by Carole

Avriett, I'm certain this will be another favorite for readers who love military history stories.

—Merritt A. Edson III

Harry Bauer Tribute

In a much earlier time in my life, my father once revealed a small book to me that he had always kept in his own father's chest of drawers. It was small and unassuming with a simple pale olive green cover and worn corners. It had a dark green cloth-clad spine, and revealed no title or words on its cover, but it seemed there was something kept between its pages for safekeeping. My great-uncles, great-granddads, granddads, and father had served in the Spanish American War, the Philippines, Nicaragua, World War Two, and Vietnam, so there were always detailed photos, historical books, and small coveted mementos in drawers and well-worn locker boxes. These keepsakes documented those times they had been called halfway around the world to serve their country, and as with any tales passed down from father to son, I was eager to see what stories were in this small book and where it had come from.

As my dad opened this simple journal, the first thing I noticed was a small piece of the hoist of a flag, maybe five to six inches in length and still containing a single brass grommet. Its faint cotton threads of white and red led me to believe that it was the remains of an American flag. My dad then said that this journal was the logbook of my great-uncle, Commander Harry Bauer, who had served in the Pacific during World War Two.

Dad told me that he had commanded the USS *Gregory* and during a fierce firefight with a Japanese destroyer, his APD had been severely damaged, and that Uncle Harry had gone down with his ship. My dad showed this little book to me only once and I wish I had spent more time reading those minute details of daily life, activities, and the courses of action on the USS *Gregory*. I never had the chance to open those pages again and I had assumed that the little piece of flag hoist was from the actual flag that had flown on the USS *Gregory* and placed in those pages sometime after. In later years I learned more of my family's military history and the details of that violent night back in 1942.

I was fortunate growing up as my father was a Marine Corps colonel who taught me the wisdom of honesty and truth, and the challenges of hard work. Dad was also a painter and illustrator who taught me about the visual world around me and always championed my conviction to create my own creative path. History is full of men and women who have chosen to walk the path of selflessness and determination, often heading towards an uncertain outcome. Though I was never able to meet my great-uncle Harry and talk with him about what he had aspired to be, I will always think about those descriptions of his selfless leadership, relentless fighting spirit, and the courage of those brave men he fought and perished with so long ago in the South Pacific.

—by Bryan Condra, great-nephew of Harry Bauer

Oswald Austin Family Tribute

I joined the Navy because I wanted to serve my nation in the same way my father and his father had served. My father's service was well known to me, but my grandfather's, less so. I knew he had been in the Coast Guard, and I had heard he served in WWII, but both of those concepts weren't much more than shiny objects as a child. It was interesting to hear, but what it actually meant was lost on me. As I got older, I spoke to my granddad more about his service. He didn't provide much, and being so young, I just assumed there wasn't much to tell. I learned later from my parents that my decision to serve was a bit of a surprise to the family. Whether it surprised my grandfather, I'm unsure. During my college years I would see him infrequently and my "service" at that time was more about maintaining my scholarship and getting through NC State. When I actually took my oath and received my commission, I noticed that my grandfather started to open up. Maybe it was seeing me in uniform during some of my visits home, or maybe it was that my questions got smarter as my own time at sea opened my eyes to the uniqueness of naval service. During one visit, he talked to me about his experience at Guadalcanal and it suddenly occurred to me that his service was something more than the average sailor experiences. Just how unique, I continue to uncover to this day. Whatever happened to my granddad after he came home from the war, he experienced what few can ever even comprehend. Naval combat is harsh, bloody, terrifying, and there are no monuments to battles whether lost or won. There is just a watery grave for those lost on the *Gregory*, and for those that survived, a lifetime of post-traumatic stress disorder that the nation didn't know how to treat. My granddad was a hero in every sense of the word. A man with faults, no doubt, but also a man who answered the call when the nation went to war. In the fiery inferno that was the loss of the *Gregory*, he honored our nation and did his duty. I wish I'd had more time to talk to him about those days at war. Bravo Zulu, you will always be a hero in my eyes.

—by grandson Spencer Austin, Captain, USN (ret)

Endnotes

Chapter 2, Part 1:
General background: *Texas Monthly*, Travel & Outdoors, "The Meanest River," Jan Reid, July 1988.
Interviews with mayor and staff in Foreman, Arkansas.

Chapter 2, Part 2:
For more information on Spanish explorers—Brittanica Online, "Ferdinand Magellan: Portuguese Explorer."

Chapter 3, Part 1:
General background: history.navy.mil—"The United States Naval Academy, 1845–2020"

Chapter 3, Part 2:
General background: Encyclopediaofarkansas.net, "Foreman (Little River County)"
ualrexhibits.org, "The Great Depression in Arkansas"

Chapter 4:

General background:

Nebraskastudies.org: the 1980 NET Television program *Legacies of World War II*

NavSource Online: Service Photo Archive, USS *New Orleans*

NavSource Online: Service Photo Archive, USS *Antares* (AKS-3)

Chapter 5:

"On 1 February 1939, Manley carried out her first landing exercise. With final modifications, the Marines requested more fast transports and five flush-deck destroyers were pulled out of 'moth balls' and converted. On 2 August 1940, the officially designated APDs, Manley APD1, Colhoun APD2, Gregory APD3, Little APD4, McKean APD5 and Stringham APD6 were formed into Transport Division Twelve—TRANSDIV 12— and the rest is history." *The Famed Green Dragons: the Four Stack APDs, APD Destroyer Sailors of WWII*, 10)

Chapter 20

For a detailed account of Edson's Bloody Ridge, September 12–14, see *Marine Raiders: The True Story of the Legendary WWII Battalions* by Carole Engle Avriett.

Chapter 21

General background: Richard Frank, *Guadalcanal*, 211–212, published 1990.

Chapter 25:

General background: Interviews with Don Austin, son of Oswald Austin.

Resources

Books

Alone on Guadalcanal: A Coastwatcher's Story, Martin Clemens, Annapolis, MD: Naval Institute Press, 1998.

American Commando: Evans Carlson, His WWII Marine Raiders and America's First Special Forces Mission, John Wukovits, New York: NAL/Penguin, 2009.

Bless 'em All: the Raider Marines of World War II, Oscar F. Peatross, Tampa: Raider, 1995.

Bloody Ridge and Beyond: A World War II Marine's Memoir of Edson's Raiders in the Pacific, Marlin "Whitey" Groft and Larry Alexander, New York: Berkley, 2014.

Blue Water, Black Men, Chester A. Wright, Bloomington, IN: AuthorHouse, 2009.

Edson's Raiders: The 1st Marine Raider Battalion in World War II, Joseph H. Alexander, Annapolis, MD: Naval Institute Press, 2001.

Lonely Vigil: Coastwatchers of the Solomons; Lord, Walter; Bluejacket Books, Naval Institute Press, Annapolis, MD, 1977.

Marine Raiders: the True Story of the Legendary WWII Battalions, Carole Engle Avriett, Washington, DC: Regnery Press, 2021.

Once a Legend: "Red Mike" Edson of the Marine Raiders Jon T. Hoffman, Novato, CA: Presidio Press, 1994.

Once a Marine: The Memoirs of General A. A. Vandegrift; A. A. Vandegrift as told to Robert B. Asprey, New York: Ballantine Books, 1964.

Our Kind of War: Illustrated Saga of the U.S. Marine Raiders of World War II, R. G. Rosenquist, Martin J. Sexton, and Robert A. Buerlein, Hailer Publishing, 1990.

The Battle of Savo Island, August 9, 1942; prepared by Dept. of Analysis, Naval War College, printed by Hassel Street Press.

The Battle of Savo Island: The Harrowing Account of the Disastrous Night Battle off Guadalcanal that Nearly Destroyed the Pacific Fleet in August 1942, Richard F. Newcomb, New York: Holt, 1961.

The Famed Green Dragons: The Four Stack APDs, The APD Destroyer Sailors of WWII, Paducah, KY: Turner, 1998.

The Lost Ships of Guadalcanal: Exploring the Ghost Ships of the South Pacific, Robert D. Ballard with Rick Archibald, New York: Warner Books, 1993.

The Marine Corps: Three Centuries of Glory, B. J. Crumley, New York: Metro Books, 2002.

The Shame of Savo, Bruce Loxton with Chris Coulthard Clark, Annapolis, MD: Naval Institute Press, 1994.

Magazines & Websites

Nav. Military Sources: https://www.navy.com

https://www.history.navy.mil>browse-by-topic

Swimming World Magazine

Wardroom Nav. Papers : https://www.history.navy.mil>title-list -alphabetically (WardroomNavPers 10002-A)

Appendix A: Reference for Ship Naming in the USN

(For further study please see "Naval History and Heritage Command: Ship Naming in the United States Navy," history.navy.mil)

Ship names in the Continental Navy and the early federal Navy came from a variety of sources. As if to emphasize the ties that many Americans still felt to Britain, the first ship of the new Continental Navy was named Alfred in honor of Alfred the Great, the king of Wessex, who is credited with building the first English naval force. Another ship was named Raleigh to commemorate the seagoing exploits of Sir Walter Raleigh. Some ships honored early patriots and heroes (Hancock and General Greene). Others commemorated the young nation's ideals and institutions (Constitution, Independence, Congress). A 74-gun ship-of-the-line, launched in 1782 and donated to the French navy on completion, was named America. A Revolutionary War frigate named Bourbon saluted the King of France, whose alliance would further the cause of American independence. Other ship names honored American places (Boston, Virginia). Small warships—brigs and schooners—bore a variety of names. Some were named for positive character traits (Enterprise, Diligence). Others had classical names (Syren, Argus) or names of small creatures with a potent sting (Hornet, Wasp).

On March 3, 1819, an act of Congress formally placed the responsibility for assigning names to the Navy's ships in the hands of the Secretary of the Navy, a prerogative which he still exercises. This act stated that "all of the ships, of the Navy of the United States, now building, or hereafter to be built, shall be named by the Secretary of the Navy, under the direction of the President of the United States, according to the following rule, to wit: those of the first class shall be called after the States of this Union; those of the second class after the rivers; and those of the third class after the principal cities and towns; taking care that no two vessels of the navy shall bear the same name." The last-cited provision remains in the United States Code today.

An act of June 12, 1858 specifically included the word "steamship" in the ship type nomenclature, and officially defined the "classes" of ships in terms of the number of their guns. Ships armed with 40 guns or more were of the "first class"; those carrying fewer than 40, but more than 20, guns were of the "second class." The name source for the second class was expanded to include the principal towns as well as rivers. The unprecedented expansion of the fleet during the Civil War was reflected—as far as ship naming was concerned—in an act of August 5, 1861, which authorized the Secretary of the Navy "to change the names of any vessels purchased for use of the Navy Department." This provision also remains in current law.

An act of May 4, 1898, specified that "all first-class battleships and monitors [shallow-draft coast-defense ships completed between 1891 and 1903, armed with heavy guns] shall be named for the States, and shall not be named for any city, place, or person, until the names of the States have been exhausted, provided that nothing herein contained shall be construed as to interfere with the names of states already assigned to any such battleship or monitor."

As with many other things, the procedures and practices involved in Navy ship naming are as much, if not more, products of evolution and tradition than of legislation. The Secretary can rely on many sources to help him reach his decisions. Each year, the Navy History and Heritage Command (NHHC) compiles primary and alternate ship name recommendations and forwards these to the Chief of Naval Operations by way of the chain of command.

These recommendations are the result of research into the history of the Navy and by suggestions submitted by service members, Navy veterans, and the public. Ship name source records at NHHC reflect the wide variety of name sources that have been used in the past, particularly since World War I. Ship name recommendations are conditioned by such factors as the name categories for ship types now being built, as approved by the Secretary of the Navy; the distribution of geographic names of ships of the fleet; names borne by previous ships that distinguished themselves in service; names recommended by individuals and groups; and names of naval leaders, national figures, and deceased members of the Navy and Marine Corps who have been honored for heroism in war or for extraordinary achievement in peace.

In its final form, after consideration at the various levels of command, the Chief of Naval Operations signs the memorandum recommending names for the current year's building program and sends it to the Secretary of the Navy. The Secretary considers these nominations, along with others he receives, as well as his own thoughts in this matter. At appropriate times, he selects names for specific ships and announces them.

While there is no set time for assigning a name, it is customarily done before the ship is christened. The ship's sponsor—the person who will christen the ship—is also selected and invited by the Secretary. In the case of ships named for individuals, an effort is made to identify the eldest living direct female descendant of that individual to perform the role of ship's sponsor. For ships with other name sources, it is customary to honor the wives of senior naval officers or public officials.

In 1907 President Theodore Roosevelt issued an executive order that established the present usage:

> In order that there shall be uniformity in the matter of designating naval vessels, it is hereby directed that the official designation of vessels of war, and other vessels of the Navy of the United States, shall be the name of such vessel, preceded

by the words, United States Ship, or the letters U.S.S., and by
no other words or letters.

— Executive Order 549, January 8, 1907

Today's Navy regulations define the classification and status of naval
ships and craft:

1. The Chief of Naval Operations shall be responsible for . . .
   the assignment of classification for administrative purposes
   to water-borne craft and the designation of status for each
   ship and service craft. . . .
2. Commissioned vessels and craft shall be called "United
   States Ship" or "U.S.S."
3. Civilian manned ships, of the Military Sealift Command or
   other commands, designated "active status, in service" shall
   be called "United States Naval Ship" or "U.S.N.S."
4. Ships and service craft designated "active status, in service,"
   except those described by paragraph 3 of this article, shall
   be referred to by name, when assigned, classification, and
   hull number (e.g., "HIGH POINT PCH-1" or
   "YOGN-8").

   — United States Navy Regulations, 1990, Article 0406

Appendix B: Brief Overview of the Battle of Bloody Ridge

(For a complete review of the Battle of Bloody Ridge, see *Marine Raiders: The True Story of the Legendary WWII Battalion*, Regnery History, 2021, Chapter 9, "Raiding Bandits.")

Five days after the sinking of the *Gregory* and the *Little*, on the morning of September 10, 1942, Col. Merritt Edson ordered his Raiders to saddle up. They were to break camp at the Coconut Grove and move to a place he called "a rest area." Those Raiders nearest him when the order was issued noticed once again the ever-so-slight, inscrutable grin. Then a few saw him asking men to scrounge up any and all available barbed wire. Something was up, they knew it.

And indeed, something did loom on the horizon—the stuff legends are made from. Henderson Field needed to be secured, and General Vandegrift was running out of options. The Japanese continued to hinder a complete securing of the airfield so critical to US forces trying to occupy Guadalcanal. He called on the 1st Marine Raider Battalion to take up positions on a ridge overlooking the field and beat back the Japanese forces attempting to retake it.

Edson led his Raiders up onto the high ridge, topped by a large flat area, the entire geographical feature shaped roughly like a shark gliding through water. Once the Raiders were positioned in shallow foxholes atop the ridge, they waited. The melee beginning on September 12 resulted in thirty-six straight hours of a descent into hell. Raiders were outnumbered three to one and at times, the fighting was hand-to-hand.

But by the time a pale dawn broke early on the morning of September 14, piles of dead enemy soldiers could be seen covering the Ridge, interspersed with Raiders who had given their all. Edson's Raiders had stood the test of twelve determined assaults, and had defended the critically important airstrips. These amazing warriors had been determined they would not be moved back in defense of the field so pivotal in establishing a foothold in the Solomon Islands. Guadalcanal was now more firmly in the control of US forces.

When the full explosion of dawn turned fiery, "Red Mike" Edson rang up Colonel Jerry Thomas back at Division Headquarters. His message was simple: "We can hold."

The Battle of Bloody Ridge, often referred to as Edson's Bloody Ridge, or simply as an iconic moniker to those who know, "The Ridge," secured the continuation of air cover for troops fighting for ground control. Had the Raiders yielded, the lack of air cover might have meant the loss of the battle for Guadalcanal. "Such a reversal would have had a grave impact on the course of the war and the future of the Corps."

In the weeks and months following, "Red Mike" Edson was awarded the Medal of Honor as well as Major Ken Bailey. The Navy Cross, second only to the Medal of Honor for esteeming courage and bravery, was awarded to fourteen Raiders. This meant that over the thirty-six-hour battle, individual Raiders merited Navy Crosses at the rate of one every couple of hours or so. Ironically, there were so many who displayed outstanding courage among the Raiders during their existence that the twenty ships named after individual 1st Raiders in the months and years to come didn't include any from the group except for Edson himself.

Had it not been for the dependable transport ships known as APDs, such as the *Gregory*, the Raiders would never have made these important dates in history.

Appendix C: US Navy Ships in Operation Watchtower, the Invasion of Guadalcanal, August 7, 1942:

US Navy combat ships:
3 aircraft carriers:
Saratoga, Capt. DeWitt C. Ramsey
Enterprise, Capt. Arthur C. Davis
Wasp, Capt. Forrest P. Sherman

1 fast battleship:
North Carolina, Capt. George H. Fort

9 heavy cruisers:
Atlanta, Capt. Samuel P. Jenkins
Australia, Capt. H. B. Farncomb
Canberra, Capt. F. E. Getting
Chicago, Capt. Howard D. Bode
Minneapolis, Capt. Frank J. Lowry
New Orleans, Capt. Walter S. DeLany
Portland, Capt. Laurence T. Dubose
Salt Lake City, Capt. Ernest G. Small
San Francisco, Capt. Charles H. McMorris

2 anti-aircraft light cruisers
31 destroyers

Amphibious assault vessels:
13 transports
6 attack cargo ships
4 destroyer-transports (APDs)

Auxiliaries:
5 fast minesweepers
5 oilers

Australian Navy combat ships:
2 heavy cruiser
1 light cruiser

Group Yoke for Tulagi:
APD=Auxiliary Personnel/Destroyer or Destroy/transport
Colhoun (APD-2), Lt. George B. Madden
Gregory (APD-3), Lt. Cmdr. Harry F. Bauer
Little (APD-4), Lt. Cmdr. Gus B. Lofberg Jr.
McKean (APD-5) Lt. Cmdr. John D. Sweeney

AP=Personnel:
Heywood (AP-12), Capt. Herbert B. Knowles
Neville (AP-16), Capt. Carlos A. Bailey
President Jackson (AP-37), Cmdr. Charles W. Weitsel
Zeilin (AP-9), Capt. Pat Buchanan

11 Destroyer Screen for Transports

Appendix D: Deaths by Country (from National WWII Museum, New Orleans, website)

Country	Military Deaths	Total Civilian and Military Deaths
Albania	30,000	30,200
Australia	39,800	40,500
Austria	261,000	384,700
Belgium	12,100	86,100
Brazil	1,000	2,000
Bulgaria	22,000	25,000
Canada	45,400	45,400
China	3–4,000,000	20,000,000
Czechoslovakia	25,000	345,000
Denmark	2,100	3,200
Dutch East Indies	—	3–4,000,000
Estonia	—	51,000
Ethiopia	5,000	100,000
Finland	95,000	97,000
France	217,600	567,600
French Indochina	—	1–1,500,000
Germany	5,533,000	6,600,000–8,800,000
Greece	20,000–35,000	300,000–800,000
Hungary	300,000	580,000
India	87,000	1,500,000–2,500,000
Italy	301,400	457,000
Japan	2,120,000	2,600,000–3,100,000

Country	Military Deaths	Total Civilian and Military Deaths
Korea	—	378,000–473,000
Latvia	—	227,000
Lithuania	—	353,000
Luxembourg	—	2,000
Malaya	—	100,000
Netherlands	17,000	301,000
New Zealand	11,900	11,900
Norway	3,000	9,500
Papua New Guinea	—	15,000
Philippines	57,000	500,000–1,000,000
Poland	240,000	5,600,000
Romania	300,000	833,000
Singapore	—	50,000
South Africa	11,900	11,900
Soviet Union	8,800,000–10,700,000	24,000,000
United Kingdom	383,600	450,700
United States	416,800	418,500
Yugoslavia	446,000	1,000,000

Worldwide Casualties*

Battle Deaths	15,000,000
Battle Wounded	25,000,000
Civilian Deaths	45,000,000

---

* Worldwide casualty estimates vary widely in several sources. The number of civilian deaths in China alone might well be more than 50,000,000.

Index

U

U-boats, 154, 187–188
US Coast Guard, 62–63
US Naval Academy
    Adrian and the, 34–35
    Bauer and the, 18–20, 21
    class of 43 distinctions, 198
    and reaction to Pearl Harbor
        attack, 39–40
US Naval codes of conduct, 32–33
US Naval ships, naming of, 22

V

Vandegrift, Alexander A., 75, 82,
    89, 105–106, 131
Vincennes (cruiser), 107, 109, 117

W

Walton, Russell E., 104
wardroom, 32–33, 60–62
Wasp (carrier), 103, 163–164
Weil, Walter, 176, 177
women assembly plant workers,
    43–44